Another 1001 Motivational Messages and Quotes

Bruce Eamon Brown

ISBN: 1-58518-847-6
Library of Congress Control Number: 2003100640

Book layout: Jennifer Bokelmann
Cover design: Kerry Hartjen

Front cover photos: (Row 1) Darren McNamara/Allsport, Andy Lyons/Allsport, Elsa/Getty Images; (Row 2) Darren England/Allsport, Scott Halleran/Getty Images; (Row 3) Stephen Dunn/Getty Images, Gavin Barker/Touchline Photo, Elsa/Allsport.

Text photos: page 47 — Craig Jones/Getty Images; page 77 — Darren England/Allsport; page 89 — Jamie Squire/Allsport; page 103 — Otto Gruele, Jr/Allsport; page 119 — Andy Lyons/Getty Images; page 137 — Brian Bahr/Getty Images

Coaches Choice
P.O. Box 1828
Monterey, CA 93942
www.coacheschoice.com

DEDICATION

This book is dedicated to my parents, Clint and Mayme Brown, who are currently in their 67th year of marriage, for their great example of teamwork.

CONTENTS

PREFACE

Teamwork makes the dream work.

If you have ever experienced the miracle of being a part of a great team as either a player or a coach, it is something that you will always remember. Making a group of individual athletes into a great team involves choices that are in the control of the participants. Building that team involves believing, becoming, and belonging. It is bringing together a group of people with diverse skills, beliefs, and destinies in a way that they wholeheartedly give themselves to the team in order that both the individual and the group may reach their full potential. Few experiences can be as powerful in the growth of a young athlete as being part of a selfless team working toward a common goal.

Many coaches look at team spirit as an intangible thing that some teams have and others do not. It's the leaders' job to teach, promote and build this attitude, and not leave it to chance. Coaches must use every bit of their creative energy to develop team spirit within their players. They must find opportunities to encourage teamwork and unselfishness everyday. Though many life-long relationships are fostered through athletics, some of the greatest memories an individual ever experiences are those that are discovered when that person is a member of a "special" team. These are the teams that learned the lessons the coach was trying to teach, and which accomplished goals together that they could have never done by themselves. By correctly applying all the essentials for team building, a coach can enhance the worth of the team many times over the total sum of its parts.

"Regardless of personal accomplishments, the only true satisfaction a player receives is the satisfaction that only comes from being part of a successful team."

— Vince Lombardi

The satisfaction of building teams and changing lives of individual players in the process may be the most gratifying experience coaching can offer. As the leader of your team, you have demanded commitments and a level of excellence from your athletes that have allowed them to achieve things that they may have thought impossible. Getting a group of people to blend together and achieve greatness is an experience unique to only a few professions. Coaching is often the model employed by other professions as they try to bring a "team" of people toward a common goal. Look how many of the terms used by coaches that are now popular in the business world. This is more commonplace as businesses attempt to create a productive and cohesive atmosphere in the workplace.

The building of a team becomes an exercise of passion for coaches who love their job. Coaching a great team is the next best thing to being an athlete in that situation. The steps involved in building a team are consistent and predictable. These steps are parallel whether it is building a team in sport, business, or in life. The professional histories of most coaches stem from the teams with which they have been associated.

In answering a question concerning why a person would want to be a coach, renowned West Point football coach Colonel Red Blaik replied: *"Once in a while you are lucky enough to have the thrill and satisfaction of working with a group of young men who are willing to make every sacrifice to reach a goal and then experience the achieving of it with them. In this, believe me, there is a payment that cannot be matched in any other pursuit."*

Several years ago, I had the opportunity to write a well-received book titled, *1001 Motivational Messages and Quotes for Athletes and Coaches: Teaching Character Through Sport*. This book is a follow-up to that undertaking. The additional 1001 motivational messages and quotes presented in this book are organized within the context of the seven qualities of great teams:

- Leadership
- Guiding principles
- Pride
- Communication
- Motivation
- Persistence
- Positive attitude

If this book enhances your understanding of the essential attributes of "great teams" and helps magnify your passion for your job, then the effort involved in writing it will have been more than worthwhile.

— B.E.B.

CHAPTER 1

Leadership

- Positive Demanding
- Action
- Character and Values
- Goals
- Focus
- Loyalty

GREAT TEAMS HAVE STRONG LEADERSHIP

"An army of deer led by a lion can defeat an army of lions led by a deer."

True team leaders need to understand and apply all the qualities of teamwork to be effective in their role. They must be people of ethical character, whose guiding principles, enthusiasm, positive pride, communication skills, motivation, persistence and a positive outlook are visible in their actions for everyone on the team to clearly see and follow. They need to live the values for which the team stands.

Leadership involves the responsibility of understanding and communicating the vision of the team. The ability of the leader to identify and separate the essentials from the nonessentials helps to focus the direction of the team and helps to bring clarity of that vision for all team members. This factor allows the team to move toward the vision with increased speed.

Strong leadership models unselfishness, surrounds themselves with talented people of character, and then empowers everyone on the team to perform to their highest levels. When jobs have been done well, strong leadership transfers ownership for that work to the people who have performed it. This step enables team members to embrace the responsibility and the sacrifices necessary to continue to improve and grow and gives them ownership in the team. Strong leadership develops more strong leaders. Leaders who can share credit without being threatened create team members who want to be responsible and want to lead.

Leadership has to be able to make difficult decisions. By always placing the needs of the team first, the team will see the benefit of those decisions and will more willingly accept the outcome of any decisions that leadership has made. Leaders should never take for granted or forget the foundation of trust that has been bestowed on them.

If everything else is equal, leadership is the deciding factor in the success of the team. An in-depth assessment of any successful team will reveal the strength of leadership.

"There are many elements to a campaign. Leadership is number one. Everything else is number two."

— Bertolt Brecht

"A leader is one who knows the way, goes the way, and shows the way."

— John C. Maxwell

"The great things a man does appear to be great only after they are done. When they're at hand, they are normal decisions and are done without knowledge of their greatness."

— General George S. Patton

"Sport doesn't teach character, coaches teach character."

— Eamon Brown

"Mama wanted me to be a preacher. I told her coachin' and preachin' were a lot alike."

— Paul "Bear" Bryant

"Leadership helps hearts with a common passion become partners for a greater vision."

— Unknown

"It is still a coach's game. Make no mistake. You start at the top. If you don't have a good one at the top, you don't have a chance. If you do, the rest falls into place. You have to have good assistants, and a lot of things first, but you have to have the chairman of the board."

— Paul "Bear" Bryant

"People cannot be managed. Inventories are managed, but people must be led."

— Ross Perot

"A commander will command."

— General George S. Patton

"The only safe ship in a storm is leadership."

— Faye Wattleton

"When placed in charge, take control."

— Gen. H. Norman Schwarzkopf

"A leader knows what's best to do; a manager knows merely how best to do it."

— Ken Adelman

"Leadership is the wise use of power. Power is the capacity to translate intention into reality and sustain it."

— Warren Bennis

"If anything goes bad, I did it. If anything goes semi-good, we did it. If anything goes really good, then you did it. That is all it takes to get people to win football games for you."

— Paul "Bear" Bryant

"To manage or to coach. People will manage the work. By attempting to manage people you are limiting their potential. A manager is a title, it does not guarantee success. Coaching is action, not a title, and actions will result in successes!"

— Catherine Pulsifer

"Faith in oneself, is the best and safest course."

— Michelangelo

"The ultimate leader is one who is willing to develop people to the point that they eventually surpass him or her in knowledge and ability."

— Fred. A. Manske

"Do everything you ask of those in your command."

— General George S. Patton

"A man who wants to lead the orchestra must turn his back on the crowd."

— James Crook

"I know no better person to be the face and voice of American diplomacy. His directness of speech, his towering integrity, his deep respect for our democracy, and his soldier's sense of duty."

— George W. Bush *speaking of Colin Powell*

"The man who follows the crowd will never be followed by the crowd."

— R.S. Donnell

"In really good companies, you have to lead. You have to come up with big ideas and express them forcefully. Over time, I came to see that waiting to discover which way the way the wind was blowing is an excellent way to learn how to be a follower."

— Roger Enrico

"There is no necessary connection between the desire to lead, and the ability to lead, and even less the ability to lead somewhere that will be an advantage of the led."

— Bergan Evans

"Delegating work works, provided the one delegating works too."

— Robert Half

"There is great force in a gentle command."

— George Herbert

"Leaders create an environment in which everyone has the opportunity to do work which matches his potential capacity."

— Elliott Jaques

"Morale is faith in the man at the top."

— Albert S. Johnson

"The shepherd always tries to persuade the sheep that their interests and his own are the same."

— Henri B. Stendhal

"The wicked leader is he who the people despise.
The good leader is he who the people revere.
The great leader is he who the people say, 'We did it ourselves.'"

— Lao Tzu

"There is no such thing as a perfect leader either in the past or present, in China or elsewhere. If there is one, he is only pretending, like a pig inserting scallions into its nose in an effect to look like an elephant."

— Liu Shao-Ch'I

"Leadership is the other side of the coin of loneliness, and he who is a leader must always act alone. And acting alone, accept everything alone."

— Ferdinand E. Marcos

"A leader who doesn't hesitate before he sends his nation into battle is not fit to be a leader."

— Golda Meir

"People ask the difference between a leader and a boss. The leader works in the open, and the boss in covert. The leader leads, and the boss drives."

— Theodore Roosevelt

"The best leaders are those most interested in surrounding themselves with assistants and associates smarter than they are. They are frank in admitting this and we are willing to pay for such talents."

— Amos Parrish

"We herd sheep, we drive cattle, we lead people. Lead me, follow me, or get out of the way."

— General George S. Patton

"The challenge of leadership is to be strong, but not rude; be kind, but not weak; be bold, but not bully; be thoughtful, but not lazy; be humble, but not timid; be proud, but not arrogant; have humor, but without folly."

— Jim Rohn

"It is a great pity when the one who should be the head figure is a mere figurehead."

— Charles Haddon Spurgeon

"Never fight a battle when nothing is gained from winning."

— General George S. Patton

"You are not a leader because you have the title of manager. Leadership is something that we earn from followers on a day-to-day basis."

— The EMS Manager Newsletter

Leadership on great teams requires:

- Being both positive and demanding
- Willingness to take action
- Having personal character and values, so leadership is ethical
- Setting and achieving goals
- Developing a focus
- Giving and receiving loyalty

POSITIVE DEMANDING LEADERSHIP

- **Coaching leadership needs to be both positive and demanding.**

"Young people need models, not critics."

— John Wooden

One of the best terms for describing the characteristics for good leadership in athletics is **positive demanding**. Things that are really important have a sense of urgency. Leaders do not waste their energy and attention on matters beyond their control or that are not essential for team success. They are demanding without being demeaning. They are relaxed and confident, while maintaining a naturally competitive personality. They focus positively and aggressively on factors that they can influence and do not worry about circumstances over which they have no control.

Positive leaders are able to recognize when people are doing things well and reinforce the action or behavior. They focus on what kids CAN do, rather than on what they cannot do. They continue to work to have their athletes improve their weaknesses, while constantly stressing their strengths. Positive leaders also have a manner that expects and accepts only all-out effort. These leaders demand and receive the best from each member of their team.

Leaders are either confidence builders or confidence cutters. Athletes, like most other people, are in greater need of your praise when they try and fail, than when they try and succeed. Make sure that your team members know they are working with you, not for you. Real leadership is needed and revealed during times of adversity. Rather than dwell on failures, good leadership highlights talents and accomplishments, provides positive feedback, and in doing so, breeds confident teams. Leaders have a quiet inner confidence, based on readiness and the ability to prepare others. True confidence is gained from productive preparation and is spread by confident leadership.

- **Great teams have quality leadership from their team members. The most talented players need to be the best workers and also have a teachable spirit.**

A teachable spirit simply means that athletes have learned to take correction as a compliment and that the coach believes in them and cares that they reach their full potential. If your most talented players are not your best workers, you will never have a great team. When a coach treats players with a low effort the same as those with high effort, the message sent to every member of your team is that high effort is not important or essential for success.

On some teams, a player may be a leader; on others, that individual may be a team member or role player. Whenever possible, the coach turns some of the leadership over to qualified team members. Some years, the coach must assume all of the leadership responsibilities. This situation is not as effective or fun. It requires a lot of extra energy and can lead to coaching burnout. Having athletes take ownership of the team teaches them to fill a responsibility role for the team, and also enables the coach to reach other goals.

"People are eternally divided into two classes, the believer, builder, and praiser, and the unbeliever, destroyer and critic."

— John Ruskin

"Confidence is contagious. So is lack of confidence."

— Unknown

"A good coach will make his players see what they can be rather than what they are."

— Ara Parseghian

"Is it the nature of man to rise to greatness if greatness is expected of him?"

— John Steinbeck

"He who believes is strong; he who doubts is weak.
Strong convictions precede great actions."

— James Freeman Clarke

"Tell a person they are brave and you help them become so."

— Thomas Carlyle

"Self-confidence is the first requisite to great undertakings."

— Samuel Johnson

"Outstanding leaders appeal to the hearts of their followers, not their minds."

— Unknown

"The leader seeks to communicate his vision to his followers. He captures their attention with his optimistic intuition of possible solutions to their needs. He influences them by the dynamism of his faith. He demonstrates confidence that the challenge can be met, the need resolved, the crisis overcome."

— John Haggett

"My father gave me the greatest gift anyone could give another person, he believed in me."

— Jim Valvano

LEADERSHIP IS ACTION

- **Leaders focus on the things that need to be done and do them.**

"Leap, and the net will appear."

— Julie Cameron

Leaders cannot be afraid to lead or to change when needed. They do not shy away from challenges or responsibility. Leaders go the extra mile for their team, doing more than is expected. They refuse to exist in a climate of apathy or less than best effort. They do not second-guess themselves on decisions made with integrity, thoughtful intelligence, and with the heart of the team placed first.

Leaders who accomplish the most take chances and take action. While their willingness to take calculated risks may involve making mistakes, without the risk of making mistakes, few growth opportunities exist. The cost of remaining comfortable with the status quo is far greater than taking action and failing.

When conflict arises, leaders are able to manage it quickly and effectively. As a result, the team is able to maintain its confidence, energy, and collective power. When real change is needed in an athletic situation, it does not require consensus. A leader who sees that a change is needed does not have to receive the approval of everyone involved to create the change. A coach who inherits players whose behavior is poor does not have to get the approval of the players to get them to behave correctly.

Action is the only way to bring change to what you understand and what you feel. While concepts may be intuitively grasped, they remain concepts and are not fully understood until they are taken to the level of action. Action leads to an increased level of understanding those abstract notions and then transforms them into experience and wisdom.

"You can't build a reputation on what you're going to do."

— Henry Ford

"I think one's feelings waste themselves in words; they ought all to be distilled into actions which bring results."

— Florence Nightingale

"I think there is something, more important than believing: Action! The world is full of dreamers, there aren't enough who will move ahead and begin to take concrete steps to actualize their vision."

— W. Clement Stone

"We cannot think first and act afterward. From the moment of birth we are immersed in action, and can only fitfully guide it by taking thought."

— Alfred North Whitehead

"A good solution applied with vigor now is better than a perfect solution applied ten minutes later."

— General George S. Patton

"A man is the sum of his actions, of what he has done,
of what he can do, nothing else."

— Mahatma Gandhi

"If the wind will not serve, take to the oars."

— Latin Proverb

"The great end of life is not knowledge but action."

— Thomas H. Huxley

"Commitment leads to action. Action brings your dream closer."

— Marcia Wieder

"Thought is the blossom; language the bud; action the fruit behind it."

— Ralph Waldo Emerson

"For every failure, there's an alternative course of action. You just have to find it.
When you come to a roadblock, take a detour."

— Mary Kay Ash

"A bird doesn't sing because it has an answer, it sings because it has a song."

— Maya Angelou

"No good decision was ever made in a swivel chair."

— General George S. Patton

"Three characters can be found in a man about to perform a good deed: If he says, 'I shall do it soon,' his character is poor. If he says, 'I am ready to do it now,' his character is of average quality. If he says, 'I am doing it,' his character is praiseworthy."

— Hasidic saying

"For the things we have to learn before we can do them we learn by doing them."

— Aristotle

"Think like a man of action, and act like a man of thought."

— Henri L. Bergson

"Never forget that life can only be nobly inspired and rightly lived if you take it bravely and gallantly, as a splendid adventure in which you are setting out into an unknown country, to meet many a joy, to find many a comrade, to win and lose many a battle."

— Annie Besant

"You can't aim a duck to death."

— Gael Boardman

"She didn't know it couldn't be done, so she went ahead and did it."

— Bridget O'Donnell

"The deed is everything, the glory is naught."

— Johann Wolfgang Von Goethe

"Let your performance do the thinking."

— H. Jackson Brown Jr.

"Someone's sitting in the shade today, because someone planted a tree a long time ago."

— Warren Buffett

"The critical ingredient is getting off your butt and doing something. It's as simple as that. A lot of people have ideas, but there are few who decide to do something about them now. Not tomorrow. Not next week. But today. The true entrepreneur is a doer, not a dreamer. "

— Nolan Bushnell

"Take calculated risks."

— General George S. Patton

"A dog barks when his master is attacked. I would be a coward if I saw that God's truth is attacked and yet would remain silent."

— John Calvin

"People may doubt what you say, but they will believe what you do."

— Lewis Cass

"Every action of our lives touches on some chord that will vibrate in eternity."

— Edwin Hubbel Chapin

"In action be primitive; in foresight, a strategist."

— Rene Char

"It is not whether your words or actions are tough or gentle; it is the spirit behind your actions and words that announces your inner state."

— Ching Ning Chu

" Knowing is not enough; we must apply. Willing is not enough; we must do."

— Johann Wolfgang Von Goethe

"Action makes more fortune than caution."

— Luc De Clapiers

"Let every man or woman here, if you never hear me again, remember this, that if you wish to be great at all, you must begin where you are and with what you are. He who would be great anywhere must first be great in his own Philadelphia."

— Russel H. Conwell

"The difficulties you meet will resolve themselves as you advance. Proceed, and light will dawn, and shine with increasing clearness on your path."

— D'Alembert

"For what is liberty but the unhampered translation of will into act?"

— Dante Alighieri

"We cannot seek or attain health, wealth, learning, justice, or kindness in general. Action is always specific, concrete, individualized, unique."

— John Dewey

"Just as a flower which seems beautiful and has color but no perfume, so are the fruitless words of the man who speaks them but does them not."

— Dhammapada

"If you keep thinking about what you want to do or what you hope will happen, you don't do it, and it won't happen."

— Joe DiMaggio

"Speak out in acts; the time for words has passed, and only deeds will suffice."

— John Greenleaf Whittier

"Everyone who got where he is had to begin where he was."

— Richard L. Evans

"The undertaking of a new action brings new strength."

— Evenus

"Your action, and your action alone, determines your worth."

— Johann G. Fichte

"The words printed here are concepts. You must go through the experiences."

— Frederick Carl Frieseke

"Give me the ready hand rather than the ready tongue."

— Giuseppe Garibaldi

"Every man of action has a strong dose of egoism, pride, hardness, and cunning. But all those things will be regarded as high qualities if he can make them the means to achieve great ends."

— Charles de Gaulle

"Fresh activity is the only means of overcoming adversity."

— Johann Wolfgang Von Goethe

"We will burn that bridge when we come to it."

— Nick Gorski

"The secret to success is to start from scratch and keep on scratching."

— Dennis Green

"In our era, the road to holiness necessarily passes through the world of action."

— Dag Hammarskjold

"The more we do, the more we can do;
the more busy we are, the more leisure we have."

— William Hazlitt

"The first glance at history convinces us that the actions of men proceed from their needs, their passions, their characters and talents; and impresses us with the belief that such needs, passions and interests are the sole spring of actions."

— Georg Hegel

"Never confuse motion with action."

— Ernest Hemingway

"Waffle ass is a curable condition in which a manager's buttocks are imprinted with the seat design of his chair due to infrequent periods of movement."

— General George S. Patton

"You don't always win your battles, but it's good to know you fought."

— Marjorie Holmes

"Act the way you'd like to be and soon you'll be the way you act."

— George W. Crane

"I find the great thing in this world is not so much where we stand, as in what direction we are moving: To reach the port of heaven, we must sail sometimes with the wind and sometimes against it, but we must sail, and not drift, nor lie at anchor."

— Oliver Wendell Holmes

"Act as if what you do makes a difference. It does."

— William James

"My father didn't tell me how to live; he lived, and let me watch him do it."

— Clarence Buddinton Kelland

"Somebody should tell us, right at the start of our lives, that we are dying. Then we might live life to the limit, every minute of every day. Do it! I say. Whatever you want to do, do it now! There are only so many tomorrows."

— Michael Landon

"The thought is not the act."

— Joan Ebbitt

"He who limps is still walking."

— Stanislaw J. Lec

"Next in importance to having a good aim is to recognize when to pull the trigger."

— Elmer G. Letterman

"Actions are the seed of fate, deeds grow into destiny."

— A. L. Linall Jr.

"You must get involved to have an impact.
No one is impressed with the won-lost record of the referee."

— John H. Holcomb

"One thought driven home is better than three left on base."

— James Liter

"As people are walking all the time, in the same spot, a path appears."

— Lu Xun

"I will act now. Success will not wait. If I delay, success will become wed to another and lost to me forever. This is the time. This is the place. I am the person."

— Og Mandino

"Let us not be content to wait and see what will happen, but give us the determination to make the right things happen."

— Peter Marshall

"Let us be tried by our actions."

— Motto

"It is impossible to walk rapidly and be unhappy."

— Dr. Howard Murphy

"And the day came when the risk to remain tight in a bud was more painful than the risk it took to blossom."

— Anaïs Nin

"Good things happen to those who hustle."

— Chuck Noll

"Act like you expect to get into the end zone."

— Joe Paterno

"The activist is not the man who says the river is dirty.
The activist is the man who cleans up the river."

— H. Ross Perot

"Either move or be moved."

— Colin Powell

"When deeds speak, words are nothing."
— African Proverb

"It is better to be the hammer than the anvil."
— French Proverb

"Act quickly, think slowly."
— Greek Proverb

"The dog that trots about, finds a bone."
— Gypsy Proverb

"Call on God, but row away from the rocks."
— Indian Proverb

"Between saying and doing, many pairs of shoes are worn out."
— Italian Proverb

"An ant on the move does more than a dozing ox."
— Mexican Proverb

"We are not living in eternity. We have only this moment,
sparkling like a star in our hand, melting like a snowflake."
— Marie Beyon Ray

"The few who do are the envy of the many who only watch."
— Jim Rohn

"Only the guy who isn't rowing has time to rock the boat."
— Saunders

"Be wary of the man who urges an action in which he himself incurs no risk."
— Joaquin Setanti

"It is the direction and not the magnitude which is to be taken into consideration."

— Thomas Troward

"Twenty years from now you will be more disappointed by the things that you didn't do than the ones you did do. So throw off the bowlines. Sail away from the safe harbor. Catch the trade winds in your sail. Explore. Dream. Discover."

— Mark Twain

"If your sword is too short, add to its length by taking one step forward."

— Unknown

CHARACTER – ETHICAL LEADERSHIP

"A man's character is his fate."

– Heraclitus

The character of leaders involves more than talk. Their actions will reflect their true character. Being a leader of character is the choice you make to do what is right, regardless of the outcome. Everyone has the opportunity to make choices based on truth, integrity, responsibility, and loyalty – all of which are necessary to develop and maintain character. Your character is revealed to your team every time you make a choice that involves an ethical dimension.

Leaders who are ethically grounded have a huge advantage when it comes to building teams. They will be consistent and steadfast and will place the needs of the team ahead of their own. They can be counted on in every situation to do what is right, rather than what is expedient. In a team environment, ethical leadership means being responsible to yourself, your team, and your purpose. These leaders of personal character–individuals who know themselves and what they stand for–provide a solid foundation for quality teams.

- **Great teams are lead by ethical people with character and pride.**

Players deserve and respond to ethical leadership. Individuals of character who are in leadership positions provide a model of trust, respect, honor, and integrity for the team to build its foundation. A team can seldom rise above any character flaws of the leader. Leaders whose character is consistent in word and deed create opportunities for success for everyone on the team. In order to build a team of character, team members should not have to look any further than leadership.

"When wealth is lost, nothing is lost.
When health is lost, something is lost.
When character is lost, all is lost."

— Unknown

"Ethics must begin at the top of an organization. It is a leadership issue and the chief executive must set the example."

— Edward Hennessy

"Teachers affect all eternity. As those who are taught, teach others, the teacher's legacy grows."

— Henry Adams

"Outside show is a poor substitute for inner worth."

— Aesop

"To ignore evil is to become a partner to it."

— Martin Luther King

"The old lessons (work, discipline, sacrifice, teamwork, fighting to achieve) aren't being taught by many people other than football coaches these days. The football coach has a captive audience and can teach these lessons because the communication lines between himself and his players are more wide open than between kids and parents. We better teach these lessons or else the country's future population will be made up of a majority of crooks, drug addicts or people on relief."

— Paul "Bear" Bryant

"Integrity is telling myself the truth. And honesty is telling the truth to other people."

— Spencer Johnson

"Humility in our quest for success provides for the strongest sort of sustainable leadership, and facilitates the attainment of true success. It is the core of moral character and is a surprising springboard to both personal and competitive excellence."

— Tom Morris

"Six essentials qualities that are the key to success:
sincerity, personal integrity, humility, courtesy, wisdom, charity."

— Dr. William Menninger

"Will you only have a title or will you have a testimony at your death?"

— Tony Compolo

"What you possess in the world will be found at the day of your death to belong to someone else. But what you are will be yours forever."

— Henry Van Dyke

"Nothing is more important for the public wealth than to form and train youth in wisdom and virtue. Only virtuous people are capable of freedom."

— Benjamin Franklin

"Intelligence plus character – that is the true goal of education."

— Martin Luther King Jr.

"The more things we can get kids to do correctly off the court,
the more they will do correctly on the court."

— Mike Jarvis

"When you have decided what you believe, what you feel must be done, have the courage to stand alone and be counted."

— Eleanor Roosevelt

"The biggest mistake coaches make is taking borderline cases and trying to save them. I'm not talking about grades, I'm talking about character. I want to know before a boy enrolls about his home life, and what his parents want him to be."

— Paul "Bear" Bryant

"To educate a person in mind and not in morals is to educate a menace to society."

— Theodore Roosevelt

"He who permits himself to tell a lie often finds it much easier to do it a second and third time, until at length it becomes habitual; he tells lies without attending to do it, and truths without the world believing him. This falsehood of tongue leads to that of the heart, and time depraves all its good dispositions."

— Thomas Jefferson

"Ignorant men do not know what good they hold in their hands until they have flung it away."

— Sophocles

"Character builds slowly, but can be torn down with incredible swiftness."

— Faith Baldwin

"Therefore, if we bring into view of others the marvelous sight of virtue herself, there will be no further need for our persuading words: the vision itself will persuade more quickly than can be conceived."

— Marsilio Ficino

"I have found who is responsible for your ethical poverty, and it is I."

— Russell Gough

"You are born with character; it is given, a gift, as the old stories say, from the guardians upon your birth. Each person enters the world called."

— James Hillman

"Let no one ever come to you without leaving better and happier."

— Mother Teresa

"I hope I shall possess firmness and virtue enough to maintain what I consider the most enviable of all titles, the character of an honest man."

— George Washington

"Character develops itself in the stream of life."

— Goethe

"If you were to sell your character, would you get full retail or would it go for a bargain-basement price?"

— H. Jackson Brown

"The character ethic, which I believe to be the foundation of success, teaches that there are basic principles of effective living, and that people can only experience true success and enduring happiness as they learn and integrate these principles into their basic character."

— Stephen R. Covey

"You must regulate your life by the standards you admire when you are at your best."

— John M. Thomas

"How can they expect a harvest of thought who have not had the seed time of character?"

— Henry David Thoreau

"Property may be destroyed and money may lose its purchasing power; but, character, health, knowledge and good judgment will always be in demand under all conditions."

— Roger Babson

"Education has had two great goals: to help young people become smart and to help them become good."

— Thomas Lickona

"People of character do not allow the environment to dictate their style."

— Jean Paul Richter

"It is a grand mistake to think of being great without goodness; and I pronounce it as certain that there was never yet a truly great man what was not at the same time truly virtuous."

— Benjamin Franklin

"When men speak ill of thee, live so as nobody may believe them."

— Plato

"Live that you wouldn't be ashamed to sell the family parrot to the town gossip."

— Will Rogers

"What we obtain too cheap, we esteem too little;
it is dearness only that gives everything its value."

— Thomas Paine

"If you let a child know that you think he is lazy, sloppy, untruthful, unpleasant, and thoughtless, he'll probably prove you right. Obviously, it is much better to make him stretch to reach a positive image than to stoop to match one at ground level."

— Dr. James Dobson

"The true test of character is not how much we know how to do, but how we behave when we don't know what to do."

— John Holt

"Parents can only give good advice or put their children on the right paths, but in the final forming of a person's character lies in their own hands."

— Anne Frank

"Goodness is the only investment that never fails."

— Henry David Thoreau

"Habit is the daily battle ground of character."

— Senator Dan Coats

"Character is indeed displayed in pressure-packed situations, but not merely so. For better or for worse, every display of character contributes to character."

— Russell Gough

"Be the kind of person that you want people to think you are."

— Socrates

"Every little action of the common day makes or unmakes character."

— Oscar Wilde

"I care not what others think of what I do, but I care very much about what I think of what I do. That is character!"

— Theodore Roosevelt

"Character is what you are in the dark."

— Lord John Whorfin

"The foundations of our national policy will be laid in the pure and immutable principles of private morality."

— George Washington,
in his first inaugural speech

"It is well for the world that in most of us, by the age of thirty, the character has set like plaster, and will never soften again."

— William James

"Character is always lost when a high ideal is sacrificed on the altar of conformity and popularity."

— Unknown

"The depth and strength of a human character are defined by its moral reserves. People reveal themselves completely only when they are thrown out of the customary conditions of their life, for only then do they have to fall back on their reserves."

— Leon Trotsky

"Success is always temporary. When all is said and done, the only thing you'll have left is your character."

— Vince Gill

"There is no better measure of what a person is than what he does when he is absolutely free to choose."

— William M. Bulger

"Good moral character is the first essential in a man."

— George Washington

"During my eighty-eight years, I have witnessed a whole succession of technological revolutions. But none of them has done away with the need for character in the individual or the ability to think."

— Bernard M. Baruch

"Good actions are the invisible hinges of the doors of heaven."

— Victor Hugo

"It is with trifles and when he is off guard that a man best reveals his character."

— Arthur Schopenhauer

"It is curious that physical courage should be so common in the world and moral courage so rare."

— Mark Twain

"Clear conscience never fears midnight knocking."

— Chinese Proverb

"Reputation is only a candle, of wavering and uncertain flame, and easily blown out, but it is the light by which the world looks for and finds merit."

— James Russell Lowell

"If you ask what is good of education in general, the answer is easy; that education makes good men, and that good men act nobly."

— Plato

"A person teaching and a person learning should have the same end view: the improvement of the student's character."

— Seneca

"While there are two sides to most every issue, your Dad knows which one is right."

— Russ Haehl

"Character consists of what you do on the third and fourth tries."

— James A. Michener

"Of all the properties which belong to honorable men, not one is so highly prized as that of character."

— Henry Clay

"Talent develops in quiet, alone; character is sharpened in the torrent of the world."

— Goethe

"Grandeur of character lies wholly in force of soul – that is, in force of thought, moral principle, and love; and this may be found in the humblest condition of life."

— William Ellery Channing

"Those who educate children well are more to be honored than they who produce them; for the latter only gave them life, but the former gave them the art of living well."

— Aristotle

"Character is a victory, not a gift."

— Unknown

"It is not hard to make decisions when you know what your values are."

— Roy Disney

"So much does the moral health depend upon the moral atmosphere that is breathed, and so great is the influence daily exercised by parents over their children by living a life before their eyes, that perhaps the best system of parental instruction might be summed up by these two words: 'Improve Thyself.'"

— Samuel Smiles

"Character is higher than intellect."

— Ralph Waldo Emerson

"The weakest of all weak things is a virtue which has not been tested in the fire."

— Mark Twain

"You can follow all the rules and still be unethical."

— Russell Gough

"The question to be asked at the end of an educational step is not 'What has the student learned?' but 'What has the student become?'"

— James Monroe

"Good character is more to be praised than outstanding talent. Most talents are, to some extent, a gift. Good character, by contrast, is not given to us. We have to build it piece by piece by piece, by thought, choice, courage and determination."

— John Luther

"Education does not mean teaching people what they do not know. It means teaching them to behave as they do behave."

— John Ruskin

"No change of circumstance can repair a defect in character."

— Ralph Waldo Emerson

"The strength of a man consists in finding out the way God is going, and get going that way."

— Henry Ward Beecher

"Character contributes to beauty. It fortifies a woman as her youth fades."

— Jacqueline Bisset

"There is no need to suppose that human beings differ very much one from another; But it is true that the ones who come out on top are the ones who have been trained hardest in school."

— Thucydides

"By constant self-discipline and self-control you can develop greatness of character."

— Grenville Kleiser

"If you are neutral in a situation of injustice, you have chosen the side of the oppressor. If an elephant has his tail on the foot of a mouse, and you say you are neutral, the mouse will not appreciate your neutrality."

— Desmond Tutu

"Actually, there is only 'first question' of government, and it is 'How should we live?' or 'What kind of people do we want our citizens to be?'"

— George F. Will

"To arrive at a just estimate of a renowned man's character one must judge it by the standards of his time, not ours."

— Mark Twain

"One stumble is enough to deface the character of an honorable life."

— L'Estrange

"In later life as in earlier, only a few persons influence the formation of our character; the multitude pass us by like a distant army. One friend, one teacher, one beloved, one club, one dining table, one work table, are the means by which this nation and the spirit of this nation affect the individual."

— Jean Paul Richter

"He who walks with integrity walks securely."

— Proverbs 10:9 (NKJV)

"Character is the foundation stone upon which one must build to win respect. Just as no worthy building can be erected on a weak foundation, so no lasting reputation worthy of respect can be built on a weak character."

— R. C. Samsel

"The crown and glory of life is character. It is the noblest possession of a man. It exercises a greater power than wealth, and secures all the honor without the jealousies of fame."

— Samuel Smiles

"Character cannot be summoned at the moment of crisis if it has been squandered by many years of compromise and rationalization. The only testing ground for the heroic is the mundane. The only preparation for that one profound decision which can change a life, is those hundreds of self-defining seemingly insignificant decisions make in private."

— Senator Dan Coats

"The greatest influence for good comes from those quiet folks who make morals, not moralizing, their vocation."

— Lawrence Reed

"Let us not say, every man is the architect of his own fortune; but let us say, every man is the architect of his own character."

— George D. Boardman

"People are more likely to watch your walk than to believe all your talk."

— Unknown

"What you are thunders so that I cannot hear what you say to the contrary."

— Ralph Waldo Emerson

"The dream of finding a substitute for character is still, of course, very much alive. The dream of a society 'so perfect that no one will need to be good' is really a child's dream. We need to stop dreaming. The truth is, there is no substitute for personal character and there never will be."

— William Kilpatrick

"I look to a day when people will not be judged by the color of their skin, but by the content of their character."

— Martin Luther King

TEAM LEADERS SET AND ATTAIN GOALS

"Life is only meaningful when we are striving for a goal."

— Aristotle

Goals give teams and individuals a target toward which their meaningful work will lead. Goals provide the mental picture that allows the role players on the team the motivation to fulfill their piece of the successful puzzle. Team members who can "visualize the finished product" are more likely to reach that vision. As such, visualization can be a tremendous motivator. Simply put, goals trigger the success mechanism in people. In that regard, the pursuit of a clear team goal can transcend any individual goal when the team is functioning as a unit. In this situation, the power of the team to accomplish meaningful purposes is far greater than the ability of the individual parts to achieve anything by themselves.

"A man has to have goals – for a day, for a lifetime – that was mine, to have people say, 'There goes Ted Williams, the greatest hitter who ever lived.'"

— Ted Williams

"Your goals are the road maps that guide you and show you what is possible in your life."

— Les Brown

"When we are motivated by goals that have deep meaning, by dreams that need completion, by pure love that needs expressing, then we truly live life."

— Greg Anderson

"Great souls are not those who have fewer passions and more virtues than others, but only those who have greater designs."

— Francois De La Rochefoucauld

"You need to overcome the tug of people against you as you reach for high goals."

— General George S. Patton

"Unless you have some goals, I don't think there's any way to get above the pack. My vision was always well beyond what I had any reason to expect."

— John Fuqua

"The goals you set must be challenging. At the same time, it should be realistic and attainable, not impossible to reach. It should be challenging enough to make you stretch, but not so far you break."

— Rick Hanson

"There are those who travel and those who are going somewhere. They are different and yet they are the same. The success has this over his rivals: He knows where he is going."

— Mark Caine

"First say to yourself what you would be; and then do what you have to do."

— Epictetus

"Aim for the top. There is plenty of room there. There are so few at the top it is almost lonely there."

— Samuel Insull

"If you don't know where you are going, you might end up someplace else."

— Yogi Berra

"The people who get on in this world are the people who get up and look for the circumstances they want, and if they cannot find them, make them."

— George Bernard Shaw

"Goals are dreams with deadlines."

— Diana Scharf Hunt

"The great thing in this world is not so much where we are, but in what direction we are moving."

— Oliver Wendell Holmes

"Make your life a mission, not an intermission."

— Arnold H. Glasgow

"Providence has nothing good or high in store for one who does not resolutely aim at something high or good. A purpose is the eternal condition of success."

— Thornton T. Munger

"What you get by achieving your goals is not as important as what you have become by achieving your goals."

— Zig Ziglar

"A soul without a high goal is like a ship without a rudder."

— Eileen Caddy

"You don't have to be a fantastic hero to do certain things – to compete. You can be just an ordinary chap, sufficiently motivated to reach challenging goals."

— Sir Edmund Hillary

"Setting an exciting goal is like setting a needle in your compass. From then on, the compass knows only one point, its ideal. And it will faithfully guide you there through the darkest nights and fiercest storms."

— Unknown

"Our plans miscarry because they have no aim. When a man does not know what harbor he is making for no wind is the right wind."

— Seneca

"Often the search proves more profitable than the goal."

— E. L. Konigsburg

"If you want to accomplish the goals of your life, you have to begin with the spirit."

— Oprah Winfrey

"It must be borne in mind that the tragedy of life doesn't lie in not reaching your goal. The tragedy lies in having no goal to reach. It isn't a calamity to die with dreams unfulfilled, but it is a calamity not to dream. It is not a disaster to be unable to capture your ideal, but it is a disaster to have no ideal to capture. It is not a disgrace to have no stars to reach for. Not failure, but low aim that is a sin."

— Benjamin E. Mayes

"In life, as in football, you won't go far unless you know where the goalposts are."

— Arnold Glasgow.

"Always have some project underway...an ongoing project that goes over from day to day and thus makes each day a small unit of time."

— Lillian Troll

"The world turns aside to let any man pass who knows whither he is going."

— David Starr Jordan

"When you determined what you want, you have made the most important decision of your life."

— Douglas Lurtan

"Nothing can stop the man with the right mental attitude from achieving his goal; nothing on earth can help the man with the wrong mental attitude."

— Thomas Jefferson

"Everything on the earth has a purpose, every disease an herb to cure it, and every person a mission."

— Mourning Dove

"Shoot for the moon, even if you miss, you'll end up amongst the stars."

— Les Brown

"Our goals can only be reached through a vehicle of a plan, in which we must fervently believe, and upon which we must vigorously act. There is no other route to success."

— Stephen A. Brennan

"It is necessary to try to surpass one's self always; this occupation ought to last as long as life."

— Queen Christina

"Obstacles are those frightful things you see when you take your eyes off your goals."

— Hannah More

"Whether or not you reach your goals in life depends entirely on how well you prepare for them and how badly you want them. You're eagles! Stretch your wings and fly to the sky."

— Ronald McNair

"From a certain point onward there is no longer any turning back. That is the point that must be reached."

— Franz Kafka

"The person with a fixed goal, a clear picture of his desire, or an ideal always before him, causes it, though repetition, to be buried deeply in his subconscious mind and is thus enabled, thanks to its generative and sustaining power, to realize his goal in a minimum of time and with a minimum of physical effort. Just pursue the thought unceasingly. Step by step you will achieve realization, for all your faculties and powers become directed to that end."

— Claude M. Bristol

"There is no quality which one must possess to win, and that is definiteness of purpose, the knowledge of what one wants, and a burning desire to possess it."

— Napoleon Hill

"Before I was ever in my teens, I knew exactly what I wanted to be when I grew up. My goal was to be the greatest athlete who ever lived."

— Babe Didrikson Zaharias

TEAM LEADERS HAVE A FOCUS

"The secret to success is constancy of purpose."

— Benjamin Disraeli

Focus enables both leaders and teams to eliminate all of the unnecessary distractions that interfere with reaching the goals that have been set. Developing a laser focus on the agreed upon goals is one of the key ingredients to team success. Leaders who can focus have identified what is important (priorities) and then have trained themselves to keep their eyes on the exact center of the target (concentration). Focus promotes attention to detail. Greatness is achieved through the discipline of attending to detail. Focusing is a skill that can be learned; it is also an attribute that is within your control. All performances improve when there is focus.

"If you focus on results, you will never change.
If you focus on change, you will get results."

— Jack Dixon

"Often he who does too much does too little."

— Italian Proverb

"Presence is more than just being there."
— Malcolm S. Forbes

"Nothing focuses the mind better than the constant sight of a competitor who wants to wipe you off the map."
— Wayne Calloway

"The successful man is the average man, focused."
— Unknown

"You have to block everything out and be extremely focused and be relaxed and mellow at the same time."
— Jennifer Capriati

"The shortest way to do many things is to do only one thing at a time."
— Sydney Smiles

"If you chase two rabbits, both will escape."
— Tor Waller

"Determine what specific goal you want to achieve. Then dedicate yourself to its attainment with unswerving singleness of purpose, the trenchant zeal of a crusader."
— Paul J. Meyer

"My main focus is on my game."
— Tiger Woods

"Every year of my life I grow more convinced that it is wisest and best to fix our attention on the beautiful and the good, and dwell as little as possible on the evil and the false."
— Richard Cecil

"Tony Gwynn is a great hitter because he has cultivated the kind of concentration unknown to most people."
— George Will

"Concentration is the ability to think about absolutely nothing when it is absolutely necessary."

— Ray Knight

"If you surrender completely to the moments as they pass, you live more richly those moments."

— Anne Morrow Lindbergh

"Most people have no idea of the giant capacity we can immediately command when we focus all of our resources on mastering a single area of our lives."

— Anthony Robbins

LEADERS DEVELOP LOYALTY

- **Leaders of great teams, develop loyalty**

"Regard you soldiers as your children, and they may follow you wherever you may lead. Look upon them as your beloved sons and they will stand by you unto death."

— Sun Tzu

True leaders inspire and instill loyalty with equal success. Leaders are chosen to *serve others*. Trouble always occurs when leaders forget this concept and begin to serve themselves. The two main focuses of leadership need to be (1) the well-being of the team members and (2) the task(s) they are attempting to accomplish. True leaders have more love for their teams than themselves. Whatever glory they strive for or achieve is not based on personal needs or position, but rather in service to their team.

By creating a climate where members of the team feel valued, positive connections are established at all levels of the group. Loyal leadership will never compromise their values.

Loyalty is tested most when things do not go well, and subsequent challenges may seem overwhelming. Leaders use these difficult times to demonstrate a commitment to those whom they serve. Teams that stay together and weather tough times often develop a bond that they may never have experienced without the difficult circumstances.

When team members have embraced their roles, established the covenant of great work habits, and a developed a "team-first" attitude, an atmosphere of unconditional acceptance is generated. An unspoken feeling exists between all members of the group that "you can count on me; I will be there for you." The power of loyalty is the force that brings out a team's best qualities during the time when this quality is most needed.

"Loyalty is still the same, whether it win or lose the game; true as a dial to the sun, although it be not shined upon."

— Samuel Butler

"You can buy a person's time; you can buy their physical presence at a given place; you can even buy a measured number of their skilled muscular motions per hour. But you can not buy enthusiasm, you cannot buy loyalty. You cannot buy the devotion of hearts, minds or souls. You must earn these."

— Clarence Francis

"We are all the President's men."

— Henry Kissinger

"Leadership is a serving relationship that has the effect of facilitating human development."

— Ted Ward

"If you think you are leading and no one is following, then you are just taking a walk."

— Unknown

"Loyalty binds me."

— Motto

"No person can be a great leader unless he takes genuine joy in the successes of those under him."

— W. A. Nance

"You have achieved excellence as a leader when people will follow you anywhere if only out of curiosity."

— Colin Powell

"From what we get, we can make a living; what we give, however, makes a life."
— Arthur Ashe

"No man will make a great leader who wants to do it all himself
or to get all the credit for doing it."
— Andrew Carnegie

"I prefer a loyal staff officer to a brilliant one."
— General George S. Patton

"The ear of the leader must ring with the voices of the people."
— Woodrow Wilson

"Unless you can find some sort of loyalty,
you cannot find unity and peace in your active living."
— Josiah Royce

"The boss drives people; the leader coaches them. The boss depends on authority; the leader on good will. The boss inspires fear; the leader inspires enthusiasm. The boss says 'I'; the leader ways 'We'. The boss fixes the blame for the breakdown; the leader fixes the breakdown. The boss says, 'Go'; the leader says 'Lets Go.'"
— H. Gordon Selfridge

"Loyalty means nothing unless it has at its heart the absolute principle of self-sacrifice."
— Woodrow T. Wilson

"There's a great deal of talk about loyalty from the bottom to the top.
Loyalty from the top down is even more necessary and is much less prevalent.
One of the most frequently noted characteristics of great men who have
remained great is loyalty to their subordinates."
— General George S. Patton

"To lead the people, walk behind them."
— Lao Tzu

"Show me the leader and I will know his men.
Show me the men and I will know their leader."

— Arthur W. Newcomb

"For God has said, 'I will never, never fail you nor forsake you.'"

— Hebrews 13:5

CHAPTER 2

Guiding Principles

➪ **Guiding Principles Should Reflect:**

- **Team Values**
- **Integrity**

➪ **Guiding Principles**

- **Enthusiasm**
- **Work Habits**
- **Team-first Attitude**

GREAT TEAMS HAVE GUIDING PRINCIPLES

A belief system guides and supports everything the team does and stands for. What does your team stand for? What is the identity of your team? What are you known for? If you were to produce a one-minute video snapshot of your team, what would it say? Too often, philosophies or mission statements look good in writing but are not who you really are... and do not reflect what you really believe about your team. A critical issue in this regard involves addressing what your coaching will legacy be.

A key point to keep in mind is that the guiding principles of well-grounded teams have remained the same for over three decades regardless of age or gender of the athletes, or the sport. The foundation of these programs and the underlying principles behind them are *enthusiasm*, *work habits* and a *"team-first" attitude*. Without these factors being consistently in the forefront, nothing meaningful can be accomplished.

GUIDING PRINCIPLES SHOULD REFLECT THE VALUES OF THE TEAM

"Principle, particularly moral principle, can never be a weathervane, spinning around this way and that with the shifting winds of expediency. Moral principle is a compass forever fixed and forever true."

— Edward R. Lyman

No matter what is written in a mission statement, the only true values are those that are demonstrated by the team members at all times. The strength of the team lies in the integrity of each individual member. Without integrity, teams lose trust; without trust, players do not have confidence; and without those values present on a team, long-term success is not possible. All lasting successes begin with virtuous character.

Sound guiding principles should be the foundation for all decisions. These principles should be based on moral and ethical beliefs and actions that bring value to a team. On occasion, teams and leaders must be willing to take a stand on principle, and therefore, be willing to stand by themselves. Principles give purposeful direction to the efforts required to reach goals of the moment, and to achieve visions of the future. These types of convictions bring credibility to the individuals, leadership, and the product if they can be witnessed in the day-to-day operation and work habits of the team. Values are the glue that holds teams together both in good and bad times. They are the essence of a team's identity. On great teams, these principles reflect, "this is what we believe; therefore, this is what you will see."

"You may be flexible on strategy, but must remain consistent on principle."

– Brubaker Movie

"The post of honor is a private station."

– Joseph Addison

"Ease and honor are seldom bedfellows."

– Proverb

"Honor is like an island, rugged and without a beach; once we have left it, we can never return."

– Nicholas Boileau

"Our own heart, and not the other men's opinion, forms our true honor."

– Samuel Taylor Coleridge

"One may survive distress, but not disgrace."

– Scottish Proverb

"It wasn't the reward that mattered or the recognition you might harvest. It was your depth of commitment, your quality of service, the product of your devotion – these were the things that counted in a life. When you gave purely, the honor came in the giving, and that was honor enough."

– Scott O'Grady

"It is a great deal easier to do that which God gives us to do, no matter how hard it is, than to face the responsibilities of not doing it."

– J. R. Miller

"It's not hard to make decisions when you know what your values are."

– Roy Disney

"Expedients are for the hour, but principles are for the ages."

– Henry Ward Beecher

"You will be as much value to others as you have been to yourself."
– Marcus T. Cicero

"Concentration and dedication – the intangibles are the deciding factors between who won and who lost."
– Tom Seaver

"The true measure of a man is how he treats someone who can do him absolutely no good."
– Ann Landers

"We can tell our values by looking at our checkbook stubs."
– Gloria Steinem

"The least of things with a meaning is worth more in life than the greatest of things without it."
– Source Unknown

"You must look within for value, but you must look beyond for perspective."
– Unknown

GUIDING PRINCIPLES SHOULD REFLECT INTEGRITY

"The time is always right to do what is right."
– Martin Luther King, Jr.

In former UCLA coach John Wooden's renowned *Pyramid of Success*, he describes integrity as "purity of intent." People with pure intentions do not compromise or waver from their core values. Their word is good; they take responsibility for all choices; their actions reflect their standards; and they can be trusted. Individuals and teams of integrity do what is right, and stand by their decisions regardless of the consequences or cost. Integrity is tested most when individuals are caught off guard and experience times of either fortune or misfortune. A key point in this regard is how do you respond when you think no one is watching?

"In great matters men show themselves as they wish to be seen;
in small matters, as they are."

– Gamaliel Bradford

"Keep true, never be ashamed of doing right;
decide on what you think is right and stick to it."

– George Eliot

"Nothing is at last sacred but the integrity of your own mind."

– Ralph Waldo Emerson

"Integrity is what we do, what we say, and what we say we do."

– Don Galer

"Integrity: A name is the blueprint of the thing we call character. You ask, What's in a name? I answer, Just about everything you do."

– Morris Mandel

"If you believe in unlimited quality and act in all your business dealings
with total integrity, the rest will take care of itself."

– Frank Perdue

"Integrity is not a 90 percent thing, not a 95 percent thing;
either you have it or you don't."

– Peter Scotese

"In silence man can most readily preserve his integrity."

– Meister Eckhart

"Let integrity and uprightness preserve me."

– Psalms 25:21

"Integrity without knowledge is weak and useless, and knowledge without integrity is dangerous and dreadful."

– Samuel Johnson Rasselas

"Every lie, every wrong we commit clogs the heart's arteries. Sometimes it takes a heart attack before we warm our hearts and clear our arteries with compassion, courage, and virtue."

– Kall

"Who walks in the way of integrity...shall minister to me."

– Psalms 101:6

"He who gets to the bottom of his mind comes to know his own nature; knowing his own nature, he also knows God. Preserving one's mind in its integrity and nourishing one's nature is the way to serve God."

– Meng Tzu (Menicus)

"To know what is right and not to do it is the worst cowardice."

– Confucious

"I grew convinced that truth, sincerity and integrity in dealings between man and man were of the utmost importance to the felicity of life; and I formed written resolutions, which still remain in my journal book, to practice them ever while I lived."

– Benjamin Franklin

"Where there are no men, strive to be a man."

– The Jewish Haggadah

"The quality of insight is determined by the degree of our ultimate integrity. Sound vision is the reward of maturity, and maturity is intellectual, emotional, spiritual integrity."

– Guggenheimer

"Having integrity...means being completely true to what is inside you – to what you know is right...what you feel you must do, regardless of the immediate cost of sacrifice...to be honorable and to behave decently."

– Samuel Goldwyn

"My strength is as the strength of ten, because my heart is pure."

– Alfred Lord Tennyson

"The only way you can truly control how you're seen is by being honest all the time."
– Tom Hanks

"Being entirely honest with oneself is a good exercise."
– Sigmund Freud

"The elegance of honest needs no adornment."
– Merry Browne

"No legacy is so rich as honesty."
– William Shakespeare

"Honesty is the first chapter in the book of wisdom."
– Thomas Jefferson

THE THREE KEY GUIDING PRINCIPLES

GUIDING PRINCIPLE #1: ENTHUSIASM

"I am the greatest builder in the world. I am the foundation of every triumph. No matter what your position is, I can better it. My name is enthusiasm."
– Anonymous

Great teams demonstrate enthusiasm. Enthusiasm is both powerful and contagious. It can provide the energy for your athletes to be better workers, who in turn will produce a better product. Enthusiasm can be spread. As such, having athletes identify it in each other can be one of the quickest methods of spreading the fire. Coaches not only need to be able to teach the fundamentals, they also need to be able to teach and model how to love the game. It is very difficult to excel in any activity that you do not love. What a great gift for young people to learn to put their heart into their work and to not be embarrassed to let it show. A true competitor brings these strong feelings to the athletic arena every day. Coaches need to bring their own love for the game, for the players, and for teaching with them to every practice and every game. Coaches who have a positive aggressive approach can be a model of a determined, strong-spirited optimist for their players to exemplify.

"The real secret of success is enthusiasm."

— Walter Chrysler

"For every sale you miss because you're too enthusiastic, you will miss a hundred because you're not enthusiastic enough."

— Zig Ziglar

"No one keeps his enthusiasm automatically. Enthusiasm must be nourished with new actions, new aspirations, new efforts, new vision."

— Papyrus

"Enthusiasm releases the drive to carry you over obstacles and adds significance to all you do."

— Norman Vincent Peale

"I studied the lives of great men and famous women, and I found that the men and women who got to the top were those who did the jobs they had in hand, with everything they had of energy and enthusiasm."

— Henry Truman

"A man can succeed at almost anything for which he has unlimited enthusiasm."

— Charles M. Schwab

"If you can give your son or daughter only one gift, let it be enthusiasm."

— Bryce Barton

"Get excited and enthusiastic about your own dream. This excitement is like a forest fire – you can smell it, taste it, and see it from a mile away."

— Denis Waitley

"You can do anything if you have enthusiasm. Enthusiasm is the yeast that makes your hopes rise to the stars. With it, there is accomplishment. Without it there are only alibis."

— Henry Ford

"Motivation will almost always beat mere talent."

— Norman Augustine

"Enthusiasm – the sustaining power of all great action."

— Samuel Smiles

"Today is life – the only life you are sure of. Make the most of today. Shake yourself awake. Let the winds of enthusiasm sweep through you. Live today with gusto."

— Dale Carnegie

"Enthusiasm is the leaping lightning, not to be measured by the horse-power of the understanding."

— Ralph Waldo Emerson

"The secret of genius is to carry the spirit of the child into old age, which means never losing your enthusiasm."

— Aldous Huxley

"Enthusiasm is the electricity of life. How do you get it? You act enthusiastic until you make it a habit."

— Gordon Parks

"Enthusiasm is a volcano on whose top never grows the grass of hesitation."

— Kahlil Gibran

"Success is the ability to go from failure to failure without losing your enthusiasm."

— Winston Churchill

"Those who are fired with an enthusiastic idea and who allow it to take hold and dominate their thoughts find that new worlds open for them. As long as enthusiasm holds out, so will new opportunities."

— Norman Vincent Peale

"Enthusiasm is faith set on fire."

— George Adams

"From the glow of enthusiasm I let the melody escape. I pursue it. Breathless I catch up with it. It flies again, it disappears, it plunges into a chaos of diverse emotions. I catch it again, I seize it, I embrace it with delight...I multiply it by modulations, and at last I triumph in the first theme. There is the whole symphony."

— Beethoven

"How do you go from where you are to where you want to be? I think you have to have an enthusiasm for life. You have to have a dream, a goal. You have to be willing to work for it."

— Jim Valvano

"I prefer the errors of enthusiasm to the indifference of wisdom."

— Anatole France

"Enthusiasm is the best protection in any situation. Wholeheartedness is contagious. Give yourself, if you wish to get others."

— David Seabury

GUIDING PRINCIPLE #2: WORK HABITS

"Your net worth to the world is usually determined by what remains after your bad habits are subtracted from your good ones."

— Benjamin Franklin

Great teams display excellent work habits. Success is always a direct by-product of the work ethic of your team. Teams are successful when the athletes prepare hard everyday, and when success does come to them, they attribute the success back to their preparation. In athletics, all successes and defeats can be traced to preparation. Teams that learn to attribute success to preparation become better and more confident performers. Hard work becomes a standard and core covenant of the team. It is who they are as team members. Every game is an opportunity to measure themselves against their own potential; every practice is an opportunity to strive to reach their potential. The wise coach only focuses on the controllable factors. The degree of preparation is one of the aspects of sport over which every coach has complete control.

Your team's goal should be to out prepare everyone on your schedule. Work, discipline, concentration, effort, and planning are choices. You should strive to develop the attitude on your team that practices are not to prepare your players to compete against a specific opponent, but rather a chance to cultivate the potential of the team and then play whoever arrives on your field or in your gym on a particular day.

"First we form habits, then they form us. Conquer your bad habits,
or they'll eventually conquer you."

— Dr. Rob Gilbert

"Good habits are worth being fanatical about."

— John Irving

"The chains of habit are too weak to be felt until they are too strong to be broken."

— Samuel Johnson

"I never could have done what I have done without the habits of punctuality, order, and diligence, without the determination to concentrate myself on one subject at a time."

— Charles Dickens

"The unfortunate thing about this world is that the good habits
are much easier to give up than the bad ones."

— W. Somerset Maugham

"Hard work has made it easy. That is my secret. That is why I win."

— Nadia Comaneci

"Habits are cobwebs at first; cables at last."

— Chinese Proverb

"It is easier to prevent bad habits than to break them."

— Benjamin Franklin

"Take control of your destiny. Believe in yourself. Ignore those who try
to discourage you. Avoid negative sources, people, places, things and habits.
Don't give up and don't give in."

— Wanda Carter

The more deeply the path is etched, the more it is used,
and the more it is used, the more deeply it etched."

— Jo Coudert

"Habits are to the soul what the veins and arteries are to the blood,
the courses in which it moves."

— Horace Bushnell

"One machine can do the work of fifty ordinary men. No machine can do the work of one extraordinary man."

— Elbert Hubbard

"It seems, in fact, as though the second half of a man's life is made up of nothing, but the habits he has accumulated during the first half."

— Fyodor Dostoevski

"Ill habits gather unseen degrees, as brooks make rivers, rivers run to seas."

— John Dryden

"A nail is driven out by another nail. Habit is overcome by habit."

— Desiderius Erasmus

"Habit is a form of exercise."

— Elbert Hubbard

"Once you learn to quit, it becomes a habit."

— Vince Lombardi

"Incredibly, many people continue their old life-style, their habits
even if they feel miserable, lonely, bored, inadequate, or abused. Why?
Of course... because habit is an easy place to hide."

— Tom Rusk

"Good habits result from resisting temptation."
— Proverb

"In early childhood you may lay the foundation of poverty or riches, industry of idleness, good or evil, by the habits to which you train your children. Teach them right habits then, and their future life is safe."
— Lydia Sigourney

"Laws are never as effective as habits."
— Adlai E. Stevenson

"There is an old saying that, you can't kill a frog by dropping him into hot water. As you drop him into the hot water, he reacts so quickly that he immediately jumps out unharmed. But if you put him in cold water and gradually warm it up until it is scalding hot, you have him cooked before he knows it. The encroachment of bad habits in our lives is very much like this."
— Source Unknown

- **One of the most desirable work habits is Preparation (Practice)**

How to be a Champion:

"You wonder how they do it, and you look to see the knack,
You watch the foot in action, or the shoulder, or the back.
But when you spot the answer, where the higher glamours lurk,
You'll find in moving higher up the laurel covered spire,
That the most of it is practice, and the rest of it is work."

— Grantland Rice

Practice is simply an action plan for improvement. It is a chance to rehearse situations where you will be tested before it counts. Successful coaches, athletes, and teams prepare for every potential situation so they are not surprised in competition. The primary duty of leadership is to practice in such a way that it minimizes as many unexpected situations as possible, while still maintaining the dignity of the players. Teams that practice correctly tend to develop the feeling of "we are prepared for anything, and we can count on each other." True confidence comes from being prepared.

"For every finish-line tape a runner breaks – complete with the cheers of the crowd and the clicking of hundreds of cameras – there are the hours of hard and often lonely work that rarely gets talked about."

– Grete Waitz

"In theory there is no difference between theory and practice. In practice there is."

– Yogi Berra

"You play the way you practice."

– Pop Warner

"If you train hard, you'll not only be hard, you'll be hard to beat."

– Herschel Walker

"Never let the enemy pick the battle site."

– General George S. Patton

"In life prepare for the hard and all you will encounter will be the required or easy."

– Submitted by Paul Thompson

"There's nothing remarkable about it. All one has to do is hit the right keys at the right time and the instrument plays itself."

– Johann Sebastian Bach

"A pint of sweat will save a gallon of blood."

– General George S. Patton

"For every pass I caught in a game, I caught a thousand in practice."

– Don Hutson

"Men succeed when they realize that their failures are the preparation for their victories."

– Ralph Waldo Emerson

"The best and fastest way to learn a sport is to watch and imitate a champion."
— Jean Claude Killy

"You don't run twenty-six miles at five minutes a mile on good looks and a secret recipe."
— Frank Shorter

"Practice, practice, practice until you eventually get numb on rejections."
— Brian Klemmer

"When I was young, I never wanted to leave the court until I got things exactly correct. My dream was to become a pro."
— Larry Bird

"Education is our passport to the future, for tomorrow belongs to the people who prepare for it today."
— Malcom X

"When you're prepared, you're more confident.
When you have a strategy, you're more comfortable."
— Fred Couples

"In fair weather prepare for foul."
— Thomas Fuller

"We all knew there was just one way to improve our odds for survival; train, train, train. Sometimes, if your training is properly intense it will kill you. More often, it will save your life."
— Richard Marcinko

"Good luck is a lazy man's estimate of a worker's success."
— Author Unknown

"The world is full of willing people; some willing to work, the rest willing to let them."
— Robert Frost

"I know a lot of people think it's monotonous, down the black lines over and over, but it's not if you're enjoying what you're doing. I love to swim and I love to train."

— Tracy Caulkins

"If people knew how hard I worked to achieve my mastery,
it wouldn't seem so wonderful at all."

— Michelangelo

"People who never do any more than they get paid for,
never get paid for any more than they do."

— Elbert Hubbard

"Good tactics can save even the worst strategy.
Bad tactics will destroy even the best strategy."

— General George S. Patton

"I don't know anything of luck. I've never banked on it, and
I'm afraid of people who do. Luck to me is something else;
hard work and realizing what is opportunity and what isn't."

— Lucille Ball

- **Another pivotal work habit is DUTY.**

"Do more than is required of you."

— General George S. Patton

When individuals choose to become a member of a team, they have an obligation to something bigger than themselves. Obligations and duties do not have negative connotations to a "team-first" person. They accept the responsibilities that come with making the group successful by understanding and embracing their role. Duty encompasses both a sense of self-dependence and interdependence within the team. It is personal accountability that turns into collective trust and reliability.

"I slept, and dreamed that life was beauty; I woke, and found that life was Duty."

— Ellen Sturgis Hooper

"Do your duty as you see it and damn the consequences."

— General George S. Patton

"Never mind your happiness; do your duty."

— William J. Durrant

"Character is a by-product; it is produced in the great manufacturer of daily duty."

— Woodrow T. Wilson

"Resolve to perform what you ought; perform without fail what you resolve."

— Benjamin Franklin

"I believe that every right implies a responsibility; every opportunity, an obligation; every possession, a duty."

— John D. Rockefeller

"Activate yourself to duty by remembering your position, who you are, and what you have obliged yourself to be."

— Thomas a Kempis

"What is possible is our highest duty."

— William E. Mclaren

"Every right implies a responsibility; Every opportunity, an obligation; Every possession, a duty."

— John D. Rockefeller

"If everyone does not pay the price to win, then everyone will pay the price by losing."

— John C. Maxwell

- **Another central work habit is EFFORT.**

"To give less than your best is to sacrifice the gift."

— Steve Prefontaine

No one can ask more of another person or of themselves than to give their best effort. It is one of the qualities over which each person has complete control. Effort is one of the major keys to success and represents the heartbeat of the team. Personal effort reflects a player's passion for the team and its objectives; collective effort develops love and respect between teammates.

"When we do the best we can, we never know what miracle is wrought in our life, or in the life of another."

— Helen Keller

"Champions know there are no shortcuts to the top. They climb the mountain one step at a time, they have no use for helicopters!"

— Judi Adler

"Push yourself again and again. Don't give an inch until the final buzzer sounds."

— Larry Bird

"Be true to the best you know. This is your high ideal. If you do your best, you cannot do more."

— H. W. Dresses

"When I was a young man, I observed that nine out of ten things I did were failures. I didn't want to be a failure, so I did ten times more work."

— George Bernard Shaw

"If one has not given everything, one has given nothing."

— Georges Guynemer

"What we hope ever to do with ease, we must learn first to do with diligence."

— Samuel Johnson

"Welcome the task that makes you go beyond yourself."

— Frank Mcgee

"Always make a total effort, even when the odds are against you."

— Arnold Palmer

"I want to be remembered as the guy who gave his all whenever he was on the field."

— Walter Payton

"Nothing can come of nothing."

— William Shakespeare

"Life does not require us to make good; it asks only that we give our best at each level of experience."

— Harold Ruopp

"Swing hard, in case they throw the ball where you're swinging."

— Duke Snider

"If your efforts are sometimes greeted with indifference, don't lose heart. The sun puts on a wonderful show at daybreak, yet most of the people in the audience go on sleeping."

— Ada Teixeira

"There's no ceiling on effort."

— Harvey C. Fruehauf

- **Other essential work habits include DETERMINATION, DRIVE, WILL, AND COMMITMENT.**

"The man who can drive himself further once the effort gets painful is the man who will win."

— Roger Bannister

Teams constantly have their sense of determination tested. Some teams will wilt at the first sign of trouble, while others continue to stay the course and do whatever is necessary to overcome the challenges they encounter. Determined people who have committed to the team find the will power to not be discouraged and not require constant reinforcement. They have the initiative to start their own motor and arrive at work (practice) with the right attitude.

Personal commitment is a gift each player gives to the rest of the team. If nothing else, commitment allows leadership to identify the uncommitted members of the team. If the inner circle of the team is committed to the values that will enhance the ability of the team to achieve success, it will impact the other members of the team in a positive way. On a team with great work habits, no one rests on their potential or on the work habits of others. Each player takes responsibility for themselves and feels the energy that comes from the successes and the sting from the failures. On great teams, everyone pays the price for success.

"Champions are not made in gyms. Champions are made from something they have deep inside them – a desire, a dream, a vision. They have to have the skill, and the will. But the will must be stronger than the skill."

— Muhammad Ali

"The achievement of your goal is assured the moment you commit yourself to it."

— Mack R. Douglas

"Not an inch of our territory, not a stone of our fortress."

— Jules Favre

'All great masters are chiefly distinguished by the power of adding a second, a third, and perhaps a fourth step in a continuous line. Many a man had taken the first step. With every additional step you enhance immensely the value of your first."

— Ralph Waldo Emerson

"Desire is the key to motivation, but it's determination and commitment to an unrelenting pursuit of your goal – a commitment to excellence. That will enable you to attain the success you seek."

— Mario Andretti

"It is the fierce determination of the driver to close with the enemy, not the mechanical perfection of the tank, that conquers the trench."

— General George S. Patton

"A man can do all things if he but wills them."

— Leon Battista Albert

"I believe life is constantly testing us for our level of commitment, and life's greatest rewards are reserved for those who demonstrate a never-ending commitment to act until they achieve. This level of resolve can move mountains, but it must be constant and consistent. As simplistic as this may sound, it is still the common denominator separating whose who live their dreams from those who live in regret.'

— Anthony Robbins

"The surest way not to fail, is to be determined to succeed."

— Richard B. Sheridan

"Desire awakens only the things that are thought possible."

— Rene Descartes

"Desire is the key to motivation, but it's the determination and commitment to an unrelenting pursuit of your goal a commitment to excellence that will enable you to attain the success you seek."

— Mario

"Until one is committed, there is hesitancy, the chance to draw back, always ineffectiveness. Concerning all acts of initiative and creation, there is one elementary truth the ignorance of which kills countless ideas and splendid plans: that the moment one definitely commits oneself, then providence moves too. All sorts of things occur to help one that would never otherwise have occurred. A whole stream of events issues from the decision, raising in one's favor all manner of unforeseen incidents, meetings and material assistance which no man could have dreamed would have come his way. Whatever you can do or dream you can, begin it. Boldness has genius, power and magic in it. Begin it now."

— Goethe

"Carry on any enterprise as if all future success depended on it."

— Cardinal De Richelieu

"If you don't invest very much, then defeat doesn't hurt very much, and winning is not very exciting."

— Dick Vermeil

"Never let a day pass that you will have cause to say, I will do better tomorrow."
— Brigham Young

"Never stop until you have gained the top or the grave."
— General George S. Patton

"People do not lack strength; they lack will."
— Arthur Schopenhauer

"What nature requires is obtainable, and within easy reach.
It's for the superfluous we sweat."
— Seneca

"The difference between the impossible and possible lies in a person's determination."
— Tommy Lasorda

"Resolve that whatever you do, you will bring the whole man to it; that you will fling the whole weight of your being into it."
— Orison Swett Marden

"Free will and determination are like a game of cards. The hand that is dealt you is determination. The way you play your hand is free will."
— Norman Cousins

"A thick skin is a gift from God."
— Konrad Adenauer

"There is no chance, no destiny, no fate that can hinder or control the resolve of a determined person."
— Ella Wheeler Wilcox

"Nothing great will ever be achieved without great men, and men are great only if they are determined to be so."
— Charles De Gaulle

"Strength does not come from physical capacity. It comes from an indomitable will."

— Gandhi

"Determination is the wake-up call to the human will."

— Albert Einstein

"I'm very determined and stubborn. There's a desire in me that makes me want to do more and more, and to do it right. Each of us has a fire in our heart for something. It's our goal in life to find and to keep it lit."

— Mary Lou Retton

"The resolved mind has no cares."

— George Herbert

"Within each of us is a hidden store of determination. Determination wins the race when all is lost."

— Roger Dawson

"The quality of a person's life is in direct proportion to their commitment to excellence, regardless of their chosen field of endeavor."

— Vince Lombardi

"Lord, grant that I may always desire more than I can accomplish."

— Michelangelo

"A determined soul will do more with a rusty monkey wrench than a loafer will accomplish with all the tools in a machine shop."

— Robert Hughes

"If you want to take your mission in life to the next level, if you're stuck and you don't know how to rise, don't look outside yourself. Look inside. Don't let your fears keep you mired in the crowd. Abolish your fears and raise your commitment level to the point of no return, and I guarantee you that the champion within will burst forth to propel you toward victory."

— Bruce Jenner

"Resolve and thou art free."

— Henry Wadsworth Longfellow

"The longer I live, the more I am certain that the great difference between the great and insignificance, is energy – invincible determination – a purpose once fixed, and then death or victory."

— Sir Thomas Fowell Buxton

"The price of success is hard work, dedication to the job at hand, and the determination that whether we win or lose, we have applied the best of ourselves to the task at hand."

— Vince Lombardi

GUIDING PRINCIPLE #3: TEAM-FIRST ATTITUDE

"The strength of the wolf is in the pack and the strength of the pack is in the wolf."

— Rudyard Kipling

The final guiding principle is *the team comes first* in all decisions. Teamwork is a rare "gift" that allows ordinary people to attain extraordinary results. The only rule I had in three decades of coaching was "don't let your teammates down." What does this not cover? It speaks to every situation in which athletes can find themselves. Good choices in the areas of attentiveness, effort, eligibility, and decisions on weekends can all be brought back to this single rule. It also leaves the coach with wide discretion. Having too many rules will often limit discretion and inhibit rather than assist leadership. You should be a leader, rather than a manager/administrator who simply interprets the written policies or rules. Leaders are not afraid to use their discretion to make decisions and then take full responsibility for them.

One of the most fundamental responsibilities of successful team leadership is to eliminate selfishness. Selfishness on the team level or with any individual player will destroy a team faster than anything else will. A team-first attitude allows people to accept roles that make others better. Great teams have individual players who each make their own unique contribution to the group's success. At least one player needs to have the skills to perform each of the duties necessary for the team to collectively function. For example, each basketball team must have passers; every volleyball team must have a setter; etc.

Although some roles appear to have more importance than others, in reality, it is the combination of skills (roles) that allows a team to reach its ultimate potential. Roles give players an identity. Every team member can bring a different strength to the total picture. Clarification and specification of roles aids in the acceptance and performance by each individual. Understanding of all roles must be shared to be effective. When each member understands their own role(s), as well as the roles of teammates, they will be much more productive and will feel much more able to participate to their fullest potential. As a consequence, a "team identity" will begin to be formed.

When leaders give each role equal value in the eyes of the team, leadership is more readily accepted and appreciated. Leadership will have difficulty building a team atmosphere if they place importance to only a few "high-profile" roles. In this regard, basketball is a prime example. It is obvious to everyone who watches a game that the people who score are important and therefore receive the most attention. But, if it were not for the player that made the pass to the scorer, or the player who set the screen to free up the scorer, the team would not have succeeded in scoring. Basketball, like most team sports, involves a number of equally valuable roles. Rebounders, defensive stoppers, screeners, passers, decision makers, encouragers, leaders, followers, perimeter scorers, and interior scorers must all fulfill their roles for the team to play as one unit.

Roles can either be a force that binds the team together or creates jealousy between the individual parts. If value is shown equally to every role, it is easier for each role to be embraced by every player. The more each individual squad member feels like they are part of the team, the more they will contribute. The more each member contributes, the more they feel like part of the team and the overall success that the team achieves.

Players will form an identity within the team for the positive role they fulfill, and, in turn, relish the role even more. Confidence derived from effectively performing a role within a team will allow that player to invest more energy to the benefit of the team. The power of an effective team is directly proportional to the effort each team member brings to their individual skills and role.

Just as specific roles must be established within the group of players, they must also be established for the coaching staff. All coaches must understand, accept, and fulfill the specific needs of the coaching team. Delegation of coaching responsibilities is essential, so each job is completed in an appropriate manner and is not duplicated. The head coach must ensure that every job necessary for the success of the team is done well and is shown value. The underlying factor is that the team must always comes first.

"Individual commitment to a group effort is what makes a team work, a company work, a society work, and a civilization work."

— Vince Lombardi

"People who are in it for their own good are individualists. They don't share the same heartbeat that makes a team so great. A great unit, whether it be football or any organization, shares the same heartbeat."

— Paul "Bear" Bryant

"I have a system based on the 'ant plan'. I got the idea from watching a colony of ants in Africa during the war. A whole bunch of ants working toward a common goal."

— Paul "Bear" Bryant

"When a team dedicates itself to unselfish trust and combines instinct with boldness and effort – it is ready to climb."

— Pat Riley

"Behind every able man there are always other able men."

— Chinese Proverb

"Before you can be externally competitive, you must be internally cooperative."

— Mike Fratzky

"It is not my job to look good. It is my job to make other people look good."

— Wes Unseld

"What sets apart high-performance teams, is the degree of commitment, particularly how deeply committed the members are to one another."

— Jon R. Katzenbach &
Douglas K. Smith,
The Wisdom of Teams

"Investing in the team, compounds over time."

— Evan Wright

"Our goal is not to win. It is to play together and play hard.
then winning takes care of itself."

— Mike Krzyzewski

"The best method of overcoming obstacles is the team method."

— General Colin Powell

"A champion team will beat a team of champions."

— Unknown

"In unity there is strength."

— Aesop

"The ratio of We's to I's is the best indicator of the development of a team."

— Lewis B. Ergen

"I searched for stardom, stardom I could not see.
I searched for victory, victory eluded me.
I searched for teamwork, and found all three."

— Unknown

"A team based on environment demands that you make responsible decisions; it requires you to take charge of your career. It requires you to develop excellent interpersonal skills because you have to interact at a much different level with our team members. No longer is it just you and your job."

— Catherine Pulsifer

"Everybody on a championship team doesn't get publicity, but everyone can say he's a champion."

— Earvin "Magic" Johnson

"The moment we break faith with one another, the sea engulfs us and the light goes out."

— James Baldwin

"When your team is winning, be ready to be tough, because winning can make you soft. On the other hand, when your team is losing, stick by them. Keep believing."

— Bo Schembechler

"If a team is to reach its potential, each player must be willing to subordinate his personal goals to the good of the team."

— Unknown

"Talent wins games, but teamwork and intelligence wins championships."

— Michael Jordan

"Alone we can do so little; together we can do so much."

— Helen Keller

"When two people meet, there are really six people present. There is each man as he sees himself, each man as he wants to be seen, each man as he really is."

— Michael De Saintamo

"None of us are as smart as all of us."

— Ken Blanchard

"No one can whistle a symphony. It takes an orchestra to play it."

— H. E. Luccock

"Many hands make light work."

— John Heywood

"It is literally true that you can succeed best and quickest by helping others to succeed."

— Napoleon Hill

"The achievements of an organization are the results of the combined effort of each individual."

— Vince Lombardi

"Teams do not seek consensus; they seek the best answer."

— Jon R. Katzenbach & Douglas K. Smith, *The Wisdom of Teams*

"I've worked too hard and too long to let anything stand in the way of my goals. will not let my teammates down and I will not let myself down."

— Mia Hamm

"We have always found that people are the most productive in small teams with tight budgets, time lines and freedom to solve their own problems."

— John Rollwagon

"Make my joy complete by being of the same mind, maintaining the same love, united in spirit, intent on one purpose."

— Philippians 4:2

"Teamwork is the ability to work together toward a common vision, the ability to direct individual accomplishments toward organizational objectives. It is the fuel that allows common people to obtain uncommon results."

— Unknown

"There can only be one state of mind as you approach any profound test; total concentration, a spirit of togetherness, and strength."

— Pat Riley

"We must learn to live together as brothers or perish together as fools."

— Martin Luther King Jr.

"Never doubt that a small group of thoughtful, committed people can change the world. Indeed, it is only thing that ever has."

— Margaret Mead

"Synergy – the bonus that is achieved when things work together harmoniously."

— Mark Twain

"A particular shot or way of moving the ball can be a player's personal signature, but efficiency of performance is what wins the game for the team."

— Pat Riley

"No one is superior to the game."

— A. Bartlett Giamatti

"We must all hang together or assuredly we shall all hang separately."

— Benjamin Franklin

"We can't have two standards, one set for the dedicated young men who want to do something ambitious and one set for those who don't."

— Paul "Bear" Bryant

"No matter what accomplishments you make, somebody helped you."

— Althea Gibson

"Unity to be real must stand the severest strain without breaking."

— Mahatma Gandhi

"If I could solve all the problems myself, I would."

— Thomas Edison, when asked why he had a team of twenty-one assistants

"The key elements in the art of working together are how to deal with change, how to deal with conflict, and how to reach your potential. The needs of the team are best met when we meet the needs of individual people."

— Max DePree

"When he took time to help the man up the mountain, lo, he scaled it himself."

— Unknown

"By union the smallest state thrive. By discord the greatest are destroyed."

— Sallust

"I think any player will tell you that individual accomplishments help your ego, but if you don't win, it makes for a very long season. It counts more that the team has played well."

— David Robinson

CHAPTER 3

Pride

- Good Pride
- Responsibility
- Ineffective Pride — Excuses
- Discipline
- Trust
- Competence

GREAT TEAMS DEVELOP PRIDE

"God opposes the proud, but gives grace to the humble."

— James 4:6

Neither teams nor their individual members should confuse pride with arrogance or a sense of entitlement. The kind of pride that helps build a team is a feeling among all participants that no person who is not a member of the group will ever fully understand. This kind of pride is based on discipline (focused attention and effort), unselfishness (the team comes first), accountability (everyone can be counted on), and ownership of their collective behavior. Successes are shared, trust established, communication is open, and new members are welcomed into the group as soon as they understand and accept the guiding principles of the team. A complete commitment to the purposes and values of the group exists. This kind of pride is developed when the leaders have a generous spirit that values all team members and always places others above themselves. These teams will always accomplish more than any one individual.

The good kind of pride is shared joy within the inner circle of teammates. This kind of pride can be seen in the determination of the group during preparation. It is not reserved for any elite group of people, rather it is available to any person or group who desires it and works toward the shared joy. Teams with this special shared feeling develop loyalty, respect, life long friendships, and memories.

GOOD PRIDE

The good kind of pride is a feeling between all team members that no one who is on the outside of the team can completely appreciate. It is the "shared joy" of the inner circle of all levels of team members that is based on the amount of work and preparation done and required to get where they are. They appreciate each other for the individual sacrifices and achievements that have led to their collective success. It is based on an unselfish feeling that the same success could not have been achieved without each other – an attitude that enhances their sense of unity. It is ownership of their own behavior, decisions, and choices that lead to team advancement. Often, this good kind of pride is developed in areas that require more effort than ability. The combined effort of a group, together with individual talents, can far exceed the level of accomplishment that skill alone could have taken them. Players having and demonstrating the right kind of pride shows respect for the team's leadership, the team's opponents, the game itself, and especially the people counting on them most, their teammates.

"It is a fine thing to rise above pride, but you must have pride in order to do so."
— George Bernanos

"Nothing has been purchased more dearly than the little bit of reason and sense of freedom which now constitutes our pride."
— Friedrich Nietzsche

GOOD PRIDE COMES FROM RESPONSIBILITY

"Good men prefer to be accountable."
— Michael Edwardes

Successful teams and individuals take responsibility for whatever happens. They do not blame others, or make excuses, or say "that is not my fault." They know that if they only tackle the difficult tasks when it is convenient or by being pushed, they will never succeed. These teams do the tough jobs and take on challenges on their own. When things go wrong, they look first to themselves and get back to work on the factors over which they have control so improvements can be made. Problems are approached head on. They realize that in order for the team to get better, changes must occur and challenges must be confronted. They are not afraid to analyze their strengths and weaknesses and devise a plan to bolster their strengths and attack their weaknesses, because they are driven by excellence.

A collective responsibility exists on a great team. It goes beyond individual improvement. Each team member senses and acts with a collective spirit. The players win together and lose together. They place the needs of the group ahead of their own. A collective responsibility makes them think about every decision. Their actions reflect what is best for the team. They avoid doing anything that may let their teammates down.

Although individual success is enjoyable, collective success carries with it much more power and satisfaction. Great teams embrace individual and collective responsibility. Everyone has their personal handprint on every failure and success; a single heartbeat is felt. As a consequence, the possibility of a great team is born.

Responsibility and team-consciousness are key factors on all successful teams. Team members clearly understand that their effort and commitment directly correlate to team success, particularly when they completely submit to the "team-first" mind set.

In an effort to truly become responsible, team members need to fully accept the relatively simple premise that the group can accomplish more together than any individual could ever hope to achieve. It is essential that trust is established among team members. Furthermore, respect must exist for the uniqueness of each member. As a result, encouraging, positive, honest, direct communication will be used if problems do actually arise. Great teams take collective responsibility.

"I am responsible. Although I may not be able to prevent the worst from happening, I am responsible for my attitude toward the inevitable misfortunes that darken life. Bad things do happen; how I respond to them defines my character and quality of life. I can choose to sit in perpetual sadness, immobilized by the gravity of my loss, or I can choose to rise from the pain and treasure the most precious gift I have – life itself."

— Walter Anderson

"Do not make excuses, whether it is your fault or not."

— General George S. Patton

"He who wishes to secure the good of others has already secured his own."

— Confucius

"A free man is jealous of his responsibilities as he is of his liberties."

— Cyril James

"Responsibility educates."

— Wendall Phillips

"To shun one's cross is to make it heavier."

— Henri Frederic Amiel

"People need responsibility. They resist assuming it, ut they cannot get along without it."

— John Steinbeck

"I guess more players beat themselves than are ever beaten by an opposing team. The first thing any man has to know is how to handle himself."

— Connie Mack

"You will find men who want to be carried on the shoulders of others, who think that the world owes them a living. They don't seem to see that we must all lift together and pull together."

— Henry Ford

"No man was ever endowed with a right without being at the same time saddled with a responsibility."

— Gerald W. Johnson

"If you take responsibility for yourself you will develop a hunger to accomplish your dreams."

— Les Brown

"Take your life in your hands and what happens? A terrible thing: no one to blame."

— Erica Jong

"Responsibilities gravitate to the person who can shoulder them."

— Elbert Hubbard

"When we have begun to take charge of our lives, to own ourselves, there is no longer any need to ask permission of someone."

— George O'Neil

"You must take personal responsibility. You cannot change the circumstances, the seasons, or the wind, but you can change yourself. That is something you have charge of."

— Jim Rohn

"Responsibility walks hand in hand with capacity and power."

— Josiah Gilbert Holland

"To be a man is to be responsible. It is to feel shame at the sight of what seems to be unmerited misery. It is to take pride in a victory won by one's comrades. It is to feel that one is contributing to the world."

— Antoine de Saint-Exupery

"Character – the willingness to accept responsibility for one's own life – is the source from which self-respect springs."

— Joan Didion

"If you load responsibility on a man unworthy of it, he will always betray himself."

— August Heckscher

"Man is condemned to be free; because once thrown into the world, he is responsible for everything he does."

— Jean-Paul Sartre

"Man must cease attributing his problems to his environment, and learn again to exercise his will – his personal responsibility."

— Albert Schweitzer

"Be more aware of responsibility than you are of your rights."

— Source Unknown

"You must accept responsibility for your actions, but not the credit for your achievements."

— Denis Waitley

"I know that no one can really stop me but myself and that really no one can help me but myself."

— Peter Nivio Zarlenga

INEFFECTIVE PRIDE

"When science discovers the center of the universe a lot of people will be disappointed to find they are not it."

— Bernard Baily

The wrong kind of pride can be easily seen in teams that are not stable. Their "false pride" comes and goes with each victory or loss. They lose this kind of pride as fast as they gain it. On these teams, a feeling exists that pride is not that hard to obtain and it can be achieved by taking short cuts or being better than another person or team on a given day. Too often, this kind of pride is dependant on outcome instead of process, wins instead of work habits. It doesn't last, and it isn't healthy.

This kind of pride is often confused with arrogance or a sense of entitlement. Both attitudes are destructive to the team and on a personal level. A sense of entitlement, where the participants feel that they deserve special privileges or that normal rules do not apply to them, can quickly destroy a team quickly from the inside out.

"Pride goes before destruction and a haughty spirit before a fall."
— Joseph Addison

"Pride costs more than hunger, thirst and cold."
— Thomas Jefferson

"Pride is seldom delicate; it will please itself with very mean advantages."
— Samuel Johnson

"To be proud and inaccessible is to be timid and weak."
— Jean Baptiste Massillon

"Pride is the mask of one's own faults."
— Jewish Proverb

"The nobler the blood the less the pride."
— Danish Proverb

"Swallowing your pride seldom leads to indigestion."
— Unknown

EXCUSES – IRRESPONSIBLE

"An excuse is worse and more terrible than a lie;
for an excuse is a lie guarded."
— Alexander Pope

Excuses are a sign that an individual athlete has not accepted personal responsibility or does not have a teachable spirit. Excuses do not improve performance or help a team grow. They are crutches. A player who accepts responsibility for mistakes demonstrates respect for himself and the team.

Players who are on a team that are having difficulty succeeding, should attempt to identify the reasons for the problems, that are occurring, identify methods to overcome them, and avoid allowing the difficulties to become excuses. Excuses have no value.

Coaches generally fall into one of two categories: they either rationalize problems, or they accept responsibility for problems. Those who continually deflect personal responsibility for problems seldom improve as a coach or leader. Positive, responsible coaches look at themselves first when things are not going well. Accepting responsibility unites and builds respect between both teammates and coaches.

"I attribute my success to this – I never gave or took any excuse."
— Florence Nightingale

"Ninety-nine percent of failures come from people
who have the habit of making excuses."
— George W. Carver

"Excuses are the nails used to build the house of failure."
— Don Wilder

"The best job goes to the person who can get it done without
passing the buck or coming back with excuses."
— Napoleon Hill

"He who is good for making excuses is seldom good for anything else."
— Benjamin Franklin

"People with integrity do what they say they are going to do. Others have excuses."
— Dr. Laura Schlessinger

"Don't look for excuses to lose, look for excuses to win."
— Chi Chi Rodriguez

GOOD PRIDE COMES FROM DISCIPLINE

"He who lives without discipline dies without honor."

— Proverb

Discipline is involved in all team successes. Discipline is not a negative term. As such, it should not have a negative connotation to an athlete. Very simply, discipline is focused attention and effort – an individual doing what that person has been trained to do, as well as possible every time. Discipline develops the "I can depend on you" trust. In order to be successful – either individually or collectively, sacrifices involving discipline must often be made. A great team member not only accepts discipline, but he embraces it for the benefit of the group. Disciplined athletes do whatever is necessary concerning work habits, enthusiasm, controlled emotion, personal responsibility, honesty, and positive communication. Great competitors find a way to channel their emotions and energy to lift their own performance, as well as the team's.

"Discipline = training that makes punishment unnecessary.
Fun = challenge + skill development."

— Unknown

"Temperance is a bridle of gold."

— Burton

"There is only one type of discipline, perfect discipline."

— General George S. Patton

"Self-discipline is when your conscience tells you to do something
and you don't talk back."

— W. K. Hope

"Brave is the lion tamer, brave is the world subduer,
but braver is the one who has subdued himself."

— Johann Gottfried von Herder

"He conquers twice who conquers himself in victory."

— Jyrus

"Self-respect is the root of discipline; the sense of dignity grows with the ability to say no to oneself."

— Abraham J. Herschel

"Make your educational laws strict and your criminal ones can be gentle; but if you leave youth its liberty you will have to dig dungeons for the ages."

— Michel Eyquem de Montaigne

"Anybody who gets away with something will come back to get away with a little bit more."

— Harold Schoenberg

"Better to be pruned to grow than to be cut up to burn."

— John Trapp

"Discipline is the soul of an army. It makes small numbers formidable; procures success to the weak, and esteem to all."

— George Washington

GOOD PRIDE COMES FROM TRUST

"Trust men and they will be true to you; treat them greatly and they will show themselves great."

— Ralph Waldo Emerson

One of the primary roles of leadership is to build a level of trust and mutual respect between all levels of the team. Strength of character allows trust to exist, and trust permits teams to function effectively. The ability to build a diverse group into a complementary team that uses the individual strengths of the athletes and protects any player's weaknesses that might exist will differentiate teams. The greatest compliment between teammates is to be able to be counted on, to be accountable, to be trusted. The higher the stakes, the more great teams depend on trust. Making the decision to become a member of the team means choosing to work with and for each other. The level of trust on great teams has to be earned and is apparent both when things are going well and when they are going poorly. Players on great teams can rely on each other to be at their best when their best is needed.

"Trust is the lubrication that makes it possible for organizations to work"

— Warren Bennis

"The man who trusts men will make fewer mistakes than he who distrusts them."

— Camillo Benso Conte di Cavour

"You may be deceived if you trust too much,
but you will live in torment if you don't trust enough."

— Frank Crane

"Trust thyself: every heart vibrates to that iron string."

— Ralph Waldo Emerson

"She knew how to trust people...
a rare quality, revealing a character far above average."

— Cardinal Jean Francois de Retz

"One should never trust a woman who tells her real age.
If she tells that, she'll tell anything."

— Oscar Wilde

"No more duty can be urged upon those who are entering the great theatre of life
than simple loyalty to their best convictions."

— Edwin Hubbel Chapin

"Self-respect permeates every aspect of your life."

— Joe Clark

"Self respect cannot be hunted. It cannot be purchased. It is never for sale.
It cannot be fabricated our of public relations. It comes to us when we are alone,
in quiet moments, in quiet places, when we suddenly realize that, knowing the good,
we have done it; know the beautiful, we have served it;
knowing the truth, we have spoken it."

— Noel Coward

GOOD PRIDE COMES FROM ABILITY

"You are the only person on earth who can use your ability."

— Zig Ziglar

Competence matters on a team. Not surprisingly, the collective talent of the individual players is one of the primary factors underlying the success of any team. People who have been blessed with talent should also be expected to step up and fulfill significant roles that are essential to team success. Talent that goes unfulfilled is a waste of life's gifts.

A teaching/learning process that is inherent in athletics provides the opportunity for each player to improve his talent level. This situation is a stretching process that is designed to challenge both teacher and student. It is a scenario where a daily series of small repetitive steps can lead to achievement of long-term goals. While the speed with which an individual improves is not predictable, the requirements for learning are. Gaining skills requires a solid foundation of specific, careful preparation, trust, effort, focus, and patience. The collective power of skill improvement is dramatic. If each player can make small improvement, the team improvement is compounded.

One of the significant steps of maturity for an athlete is going from the stage where having fun is being silly to a point where having fun is being good (skilled at what that person does). Within the athletic arena, this transformation happens through coaching. It is something that is taught. Athletes become proud of the ability that they acquired through effort, work habits and preparation. They show up and follow through with their role everyday. They know that they can be counted on to fulfill their role on the team.

"The person born with a talent they are meant to use,
will find their greatest happiness in using it."

— Goethe

"I will not accept anything less than the best a player's capable of doing...
and he has the right to expect the best that I can do for him and the team."

— Lou Holtz

"Hide not your talents. They for use were made. What's a sundial in the shade?"

— Benjamin Franklin

"Our work is the presentation of our capabilities."

— Goethe

CHAPTER 4

Communication

- Appreciation
- Thankfulness
- Truth

GREAT TEAMS COMMUNICATE

"A teachable point of view when combined with the proper teachable moment, makes for an optimum learning environment that can have a positive impact on the organization if you communicate quickly and at an instinctive level."

– Dr. Jim Peterson

Great teams have a climate of trust based on good communication. It is much easier to support any teammate when you have a relationship based on open, honest, and direct communication. On the best of teams, communication, both positive and corrective, is appreciated and seen for what it really is – a statement that people care for you. Good communication allows every member within the team to feel secure in expressing his views. Effective communication also elicits a high degree of support for each other and the decisions of the group by members of the team.

As a point of fact, good communication sometimes involves an athlete being corrected. On the other hand, correction should not be confused with criticism. Correction is a form of praise to an athlete in which the coach says he believes that the athlete is capable of improving. When correction is given, it is best to be done in a neutral tone and focused on the action, rather than the person or personality of the athlete. All critiques need to be accompanied by a positive suggestion for individual or team improvement.

Positive, clear communication impacts the energy on a team and makes complicated concepts appear relatively simple. By confronting potential problems early and openly, such problems seldom get to the demoralizing stage where they lead to frustration and complaints. Team members must be willing to accept constructive correction, provide honest responses, and face issues head on. When individual team members can express themselves openly, confront mistakes, areas of confusion and frustrations, they will function much more effectively. Leadership is able to learn the most by listening.

For a coach to be accurately aware of the pulse of his team, he must know what is in their minds and hearts. Talking is simply repeating what you already know. Listening is learning, and, as such, is one of the most powerful forms of communication. The key point is that good leaders are good listeners.

Before problems arise, good teams revisit and review their purpose on a regular basis. They agree on where they are going, why they need to get there, and assess how they are doing on the journey. When conflict does show itself, the team must return to its core values and realign itself with the purposes, goals, values, and mission statement as its main method for resolution. Mission statements need to be readily visible and must be adhered consistently and constantly in order to overcome adversity, as well as celebrate team successes.

Teams that have learned to communicate maturely say what they think, ask for help, share ideas, and are willing to risk making mistakes in front of each other. That approach leads to consistent improvement where the focus is on solutions. This situation can only happen when leadership has created a trusting and caring atmosphere.

Communicating acceptance is critical for team building. This task is not difficult for coaches who use verbal cues as their primary method of reinforcement. Because most players can apparently thrive on about a compliment for about a week, coaches should compliment their players frequently in order to stay well ahead of their athletes' needs. Coaches should look for the good in each player and identify things that he is doing correctly, at least as often as he may be doing something that needs improvement. One positive area that can always be rewarded is physical effort. By clearly communicating to his players that their effort to do their best for the team is important to him regardless of the outcome of the contest, a coach sends a message of acceptance.

"The more elaborate our means of communication, the less we communicate."

— Diogenes Laertius

"One of the best ways to persuade others is with your ears – by listening to them."

— Dean Rusk

"If you whoop and holler all the time, the players just get used to it."

— Paul "Bear" Bryant

"If the person you are talking to doesn't appear to be listening, be patient. It may simply be that he has a small piece of fluff in his ear."

— A. A. Milne

"Kindness in words creates confidence,
Kindness in thinking creates profoundness,
Kindness in giving creates love."

— Lao-Tse

"Constantly develop your communication skills as they are one of the key skills in life."
— Catherine Pulsifer

"When the mind is thinking, it is talking to itself."
— Plato

"Many a man would rather you heard his story than grant his request."
— Philip Stanhope

"Silence is one great art of conversation."
— William Hazlitt

"Not only say the right thing in the right place, but far more difficult, to leave unsaid the wrong thing at the tempting moment."
— George Sala

"A lie never lives to be old."
— Socrates

"I remind myself every morning; nothing I say will teach me anything."
— Larry King

"For good or ill, your conversation is your advertisement. Every time you open your mouth you let men look into your mind."
— Bruce Burton

"There are four ways, and only four ways, in which we have contact with the world. We are evaluated and classified by these four contacts: what we do, how we look, what we say, and how we say it."
— Dale Carnegie

"There are men who would quickly love each other if once they were to speak to each other; for when they spoke they would discover that their souls had only separated by phantoms and delusions."
— Ernest Hello

"Communication is not only the essence of being human,
but also a vital property of life."

— John A. Piece

"Honest disagreement is often a good sign of progress."

— Gandhi

"The true spirit of conversation consists in building on another man's observation,
not overturning it."

— Edward Bulwer-Lytton

"To express the most difficult matters clearly and intelligently,
is to strike coins out of pure gold."

— Geibel

"No one would talk much in society if they knew
how often they misunderstood others."

— Goethe

"We cannot always control our thought, but we can control our words, and repetition
impresses the subconscious, and we are master of the situation."

— Florence Scovel Shinn

"Don't talk too much. Don't pop off. Don't talk after the game until you cool off."

— Paul "Bear" Bryant

"Nothing is so simple that it cannot be misunderstood."

— Jr. Teague

"Don't hide your strategy under a bushel. Communicate it throughout your team.
It's better to disclose too much than too little."

— Joel E. Ross

"I figured if I said it enough, I would convince the world that I really was the greatest."

— Muhammad Ali

"Two monologues do make a dialogue."
— Jeff Daly

"The higher you go, the wider spreads the network of communication that will make or break you. It extends not only to more people below, but to levels above. And it extends all around, to endless other departments and interests interacting with yours."
— Donald Walton

APPRECIATION AND THANKFULNESS COMMUNICATE VALUE WITH AFFIRMATION AND PRAISE

"Kind words can be short and easy to speak, but their echoes are truly endless."
— Mother Teresa

Gratitude signifies a heightened sense of maturity within a team. It indicates sincere caring and humility between team members. Where appreciation is shown, more courtesy and concern for each other exists, and arrogance is stifled. Generosity becomes contagious, and selfishness and individual egos are reduced. Generosity is a more likely occurrence when team members are happy and valued, and leadership places the needs of others first.

All team members face times when they need assistance. During these situations, the spirits of these individuals can be lifted by any form of appreciation from the people they care about. People on a team who cannot show gratitude are often unhappy, as well as selfish with their own goals.

Positive reinforcement and praise can lead to a substantial change in people. For example, love and respect are gained from positive leadership, which in turn builds trust. Positive development occurs best in a climate of trust and affirmation. Coaches should lead by the strength of essential values and guiding principles. Communicating value can inspire the group to see the good in themselves and in each other.

"To say 'Well done' to any bit of good work is to take hold of the powers which have made the effort and strengthen them beyond our knowledge."
— Phillips Brooks

"Appreciative words are the most powerful force for good on earth."

— George W. Crane

"You take those little rascals, talk to them good, pat them on the back, let them think they are good, and they will go out and beat those biguns."

— Paul "Bear" Bryant

"Correction does much, encouragement does more."

— Goethe

Some words are like rays of sunshine, others like barbed arrows or the bite of a serpent. And if hard words cut so deep, how much pleasure can kind ones give?"

— John Lubbock

"Everyone has an invisible sign hanging around their neck saying, 'Make me feel important.' Never forget this message when working with people."

— Mary Kay

"All that is not given is lost."

— Rabindranath Tagore

"There is no investment you can make which will pay you so well as the effort to scatter sunshine and good cheer through your establishment."

— Orison Swett Marden

"You can handle people more successfully by enlisting their feeling than by convincing their reason."

— Paul P. Parker

"We are apt to love praise, but not deserve it. But if we would deserve it, we must love virtue more than that."

— William Penn

"I like to hear a man talk about himself because then I never hear anything but good."

— Will Rogers

"I have yet to find the man, however exalted his station, who did not do better work and put forth greater effort under a spirit of approval than under a spirit of criticism.

— Charles M. Schwab

"When life seems just a dreary grind; and things seem fated to annoy; say something nice to someone else and watch the world light up with joy."

— Unknown

"A man desires praise that he may be reassured, that he may quit his doubting of himself; he is indifferent to applause when he is confident of success."

— Alec Waugh

"Good, the more communicated, the more abundant grows."

— John Milton

"It is repetition of affirmation that leads to belief. And once that belief becomes a deep conviction, things begin to happen."

— Claude M. Bristol

"A compliment is verbal sunshine."

— Robert Orben

"Hearing improves with praise."

— Mark Gottfried

"For today and its blessing, I owe the world an attitude of gratitude."

— Clarence E. Hodges

"Remember that not to be happy is not to be grateful."

— Elizabeth Carter

"There are high spots in all of our lives and most of them have come about through encouragement from someone else. I don't care how great, how famous or successful a man or woman may be, each hungers for applause."

— George M. Adams

"Both abundance and lack exist simultaneously in our lives, as parallel realities. It is always our conscious choice which secret garden we will tend. When we choose not to focus on what is missing from our lives but are grateful for the abundance what's present...love, health, family, friends, work, the joys of nature and personal pursuits that bring us pleasure.. the wasteland of illusion falls away and we experience heaven on earth."

— Sarah Ban Breathnach

"Feeling grateful or appreciative of someone or something in your life actually attracts more of the things that you appreciate and value in your life."

— Christiane Northrup

"One can never pay in gratitude; one can only pay 'in kind' somewhere else in life."

— Anne Morrow Lindbergh

"No duty is more urgent than that of returning thanks."

— St. Ambrose

"Flatter me and I may not believe you. Criticize me, and I may not like you. Ignore me, and I may not forgive you. Encourage me, and I may not forget you."

— William Arthur

"Gratitude is the heart's memory."

— French Proverb

"Appreciation is a wonderful thing; it makes what is excellent in others belong to us as well."

— Voltaire

"To speak gratitude is courteous and pleasant, to enact gratitude is generous and noble, but to live gratitude is to touch heaven."

— Johannes A. Gaertner

"There is a calmness to a life lived in gratitude, a quiet joy."

— Ralph H. Blum

"Gratitude unlocks the fullness of life. It turns what we have into enough, and more. It turns denial into acceptance, chaos to order, confusion to clarity. It can turn a meal into a feast, a house into a home, a stranger into a friend. Gratitude makes sense of our past, brings peace for today, and creates a vision for tomorrow."

— Melody Beattie

"Two kinds of gratitude: The sudden kind we feel for what we take; the larger kind we feel for what we give."

— Edwin Arlington Robinson

"Correction does much, but encouragement does more. Encouragement after censure is as the sun after a shower."

— Goethe

"Those who are lifting the world upward and onward are those who encourage more than criticize."

— Elizabeth Harrison

"Gratitude is our most direct line to God and the angels. If we take the time, no matter how crazy and troubled we feel, we can find something to be thankful for. The more we seek gratitude, the more reason the angels will give us for gratitude and joy to exist in our lives."

— Terry Lynn Taylor

"I believe that many man's life will be filled with constant and unexpected encouragement, if he make up his mind to do his level best each day, and as nearly as possible reaching the high water of pure and useful living."

— Booker T. Washington

"Because gratification of a desire leads to the temporary stilling of the mind and the experience of the peaceful, joyful self it's no wonder that we get hooked on thinking that happiness comes from the satisfaction of desires. This is the meaning of the old adage, 'Joy is not in things, it is in us.'"

— Joan Borysenko

COMMUNICATE TRUTH

"Truth is always the strongest argument."
— Sophocles

Being truthful involves speaking and acting in alignment with the highest of an individual's ethical values. Communicating truthfully is a simple concept – one that involves exact verbal or visual representation of what a person believes. It is the basis for and demonstration of integrity. Truth in a team situation involves being creditable with each other through the consistency of everyone's actions. Truth needs to be apparent when addressing strengths or weaknesses, as well as an admission of an individual's own mistakes. In reality, when it reflects love and respect, truth is appreciated. Among the rewards of being truthful are that people are able to communicate clearly without deception, which translates into confidence, trust and progress for the team.

"If you ever hear a case of lying, look for severe parents. A lie would have no sense unless the truth were felt dangerous."
— Alfred Alder

"It is a pleasure to stand upon the shore and see ships tossed upon the sea: a pleasure to stand in the window of a castle, and to see a battle and the adventures thereof below: but no pleasure is comparable to standing upon the vantage ground of truth, and see the errors, and wanderings and mists and tempests in the vale below."
— Francis Bacon

"You will never find yourself until you face the truth."
— Pearl Bailey

"There's little truth in all jive, and little jive in all truth."
— Leonard Barnes

"When you want to fool the world, tell the truth."
— Otto Von Bismarck

"Truth can never be told so as to be understood, and not be believed."

— William Blake

"A few observations and much reasoning lead to error; many observation and little reasoning lead to truth."

— Alexis Carrel

"The pursuit of truth will set you free; even if you never catch up with it."

— Clarence Darrow

"Time is precious, but truth is more precious than time."

— Benjamin Disraeli

"Whoever undertakes to set himself up as judge in the field of truth and knowledge is shipwrecked by the laughter of the Gods."

— Albert Einstein

"Whatever separates you from the truth, throw it away, it will vanish anyhow."

— Yumus Emre

"A man that seeks truth and loves it must be reckoned precious to any human society."

— Epictetus

"If I had my hand full of truth, I would take good care how I opened it."

— Bernard Le Bovier de Fontenelle

"Truth is a thing immortal and perpetual, and it gives to us a beauty that fades not away in time."

— Max Fuller

"Whenever you have the truth, it must be given with love, or the message and the messenger will be rejected."

— Mahatma Gandhi

"I don't want yes men around me. I want everyone to tell the truth, even if it costs them their jobs,"

— Samuel Goldwyn

"What is, is; and what ain't, ain't."

— Joseph E. Granville

"Truth is not determined by a majority vote."

— Doug Gwyn

"Truth is a torch that shines through the fog without dispelling it."

— Claude Adrien Helvetius

"Respect for the truth comes close to being the basis for all morality."

— Frank Herbert

"The wise boldly pick up the truth as soon as they hear it. Don't wait for a moment."

— Hsuch-Dou

"The man who fears no truth has nothing to fear from lies."

— Thomas Jefferson

"No matter what you believe, it doesn't change the facts."

— Al Kersha

"Receiving the truth is like adding a new sense."

— Liebig

"Peace if possible, but truth at any rate."

— Martin Luther

"We spend all our time looking for some concept of truth, but truth is what is left when we drop all concepts."

— David Merzel

"Truth and virtue conquer."
— Motto

"Telling someone the truth is a loving act."
— Mal Pancoast

"Truth fears nothing but concealment."
— Proverb

"A half truth is a whole lie."
— Yiddish Proverb

"Truth can be a dangerous thing. It is quite patient and relentless."
— R. Scott Richards

"Truth lives on in the midst of deception."
— Johann Friedrich von Schiller

"Everything you add to the truth, subtracts from the truth."
— Alexander Solzhenitsyn

"Between whom there is hearty truth, there is love."
— Henry David Thoreau

"We must have strong minds, ready to accept facts as they are."
— Harry Truman

"Beware of the half truth. You may have gotten hold of the wrong half."
— Unknown

"One of the surest ways to convey misinformation is to tell the strict truth."
— Mark Twain

CHAPTER 5

Motivation

- ➪ **Vision and Dreams**
- ➪ **Heart and Passion**

GREAT TEAMS ARE MOTIVATED

"Every great achievement is the story of a flaming heart."
— Harry Truman

Within the team itself, a common agreement should exist concerning expectations for the team; and those expectations are high. Great teams can figuratively "start their own engine" by allowing their collective personal motivation to strengthen and build each other. All factors considered, the clearer the mission and focus are within the team, the easier it is for team members to be motivated toward a united purpose. High morale magnifies all the positives that a team experiences. Coaches should keep in mind that teams will seldom exceed the shared expectations or level of motivation of the group.

A strong *desire to succeed* among the team leaders should exist that is spread in a positive manner to all associated with the group. The levels of commitment, achievement and unselfishness, energy, and confidence all expand. Motivated teams are competitive. Competition should exist for every position and for each role within the team. That competitive nature is appreciated by the best of teams and seen as a viable means to improve the team's overall performance. Within that context, players on great teams band together to take the competitive nature that exists within the team and to employ it against each and every opponent. They look forward to the toughest of competition and focus their preparation toward that vision.

Prepare every practice for the best team their team will play against. Motivation can come from within each person or from the outside. Teams are most effective when they are motivated by both sources.

"Leadership is the ability to lift and inspire."
— Paul Dietzel

In sport, as in life, either hope of achieving a particular benefit or fear of experiencing a specific consequence triggers most motivation. As a rule, it's true that most individuals coach as they were coached as athletes. For example, if individuals grew up with coaches who used fear as the primary motivator, they typically begin their coaching career using the same tactic. It is a fact that fear works as a motivator (to a degree). While fear works, it does not function nearly as well as love and respect. Love and respect bring a deeper purpose to the level of motivation. A team motivated through love and respect produces great memories and lasting friendships. Tasks are completed, discipline accepted, expectations increased because teammates do not want to let each other down. They depend on and trust one another to complete their mission. Each role on a team tends to become equal in value on a team where individuals value each other.

Self-motivation is essential for team success. The most successful team leaders have the ability to create conditions where the participants motivate and drive themselves. These leaders can make others see the best in themselves and build on those strengths.

Teams that are made up of needy individuals who require other people to get them going do not tend to hold up in the long days of practice or in the toughest of times that occur during a season. They eventually succumb to the attendant pressures or require so much attention that they get left behind.

In reality, some sports only attract self-directed participants. Athletes who require external motivation to work hard do not survive in sports where success is based on a lot of solitary training (like cross-country and swimming) – training that involves a lot of self discipline and initiative. As such, if any athlete consistently depends on some other source for his motivation, he is seldom able to sustain his focus, effort or drive, and eventually can become an energy drag on the team.

Motivated teams work in an atmosphere of openness. They are not afraid to hustle, to try, to ask for help, or even to fail in front of each other. They are bound together by the same love and respect their leader has for them. Love of team, the sport, and the sense of competition binds them together.

One of the measuring sticks for the differences between teams is how long teams remain motivated and what it takes to stifle their motivation. In fact, motivation can be curbed. All other factors being equal, a team that can go through failure or difficult times and maintain its high level of expectations and motivation will have a much greater chance of success than the group that gets discouraged at the first sign of a problem. Teams that have developed sincere friendship, camaraderie, and loyalty can withstand troubles easier than groups that have not developed those types of relationships. This factor too is often a reflection of leadership (both coaches and players).

Teams motivated by fear not only get discouraged easier but also can become resentful of the leader who is imposing the fear. On teams where fear has been used as the primary form of motivation and punishment is given for mistakes, players will tend to avoid taking on any responsibility in order to prevent making mistakes and receiving the anticipated punishment. Teams built around love, respect, and group responsibility lean on each other in times of trouble and tend to be able to sustain their motivation for longer periods of time. Individually they have learned to be an active participant in their own rescue and collectively. As such, they will not allow each other to get down.

"From a little spark may burst a mighty flame."

— Dante

"You have to learn what makes Sammy run. For one player it is a pat on the back, for another it's chewing him out, for still another it's a fatherly talk. You are a fool if you think as I did as a young coach, that you can treat them all alike."

— Paul "Bear" Bryant

"Strong lives are motivated by dynamic purposes;
lesser ones exist on wishes and inclinations."

— Kenneth Hildebrand

"Fun helps remove the barriers that allow people to motivate themselves."

— Herman Cain

"If you want to build a ship, don't drum up people to collect wood and don't assign them tasks and work, but rather teach them to long for the endless immensity of the sea."

— Antoine de Saint-Exupery

"A message prepared in the mind reaches a mind;
a message prepared in a life reaches a life."

— Ken Gilbert

"Keep your fears to yourself, but share your inspiration with others."

— Robert Louis Stevenson

"Motivation is what gets you started. Habit is what keeps you going."

— Jim Ryun

"A man paints with his brains and not with his hands."

— Michelangelo

"What we see depends mainly on what we look for."

— Sir John Lubbock

"The best morale exists when you never hear a word mentioned. When you hear a lot of talk about it, it's usually lousy."

— Dwight D. Eisenhower

"People who are unable to motivate themselves must be content with mediocrity, no matter how impressive their other talents."

— Andrew Carnegie

"Motivation is a fire from within. If someone else tries to light that fire under you, chances are it will burn very briefly."

— Stephen R. Covey

"When the administrator feels himself to be the sole driving agency, and finds himself chiefly engaged in arousing those who are apathetic and coercing those who are antagonistic, there is something vitally wrong with the administration."

— E.E Jones

"Mr. Scorpio says productivity is up 2% and it's all because of my motivational techniques, like doughnuts, and the possibility of more doughnuts to come."

— Homer Simpson

"People often say that motivation doesn't last. Well, neither does bathing, that is why we recommend it daily."

— Zig Ziglar

"When we are motivated by goals that have deep meaning, by dreams that need competition, by pure love that needs expressing, then we truly live life."

— Greg Anderson

"Do not quench your inspiration and your imagination; do not become the slave of your model."

— Vincent Van Gogh

"Motivation is everything. You can do the work of two people, but you can't be two people. Instead, you have to inspire the next guy down the line and get him to inspire his people."

— Lee Iacocca

MOTIVATE THROUGH VISION AND DREAMS

- **Leaders must see the big picture.**

"All men of action are dreamers."

— James G. Huneker

Leaders have responsibility for understanding and sharing a clear vision to their team. The clearer the vision is to leadership, the easier they can formulate that vision to the team. The vision and goals of a team must be mutually beneficial, meeting the needs and adding value to all. Individuals must be able to see their role is essential, but that the specific goal of the team is more important than their individual role.

While a vision usually starts with a single person, great leaders are capable of consistently moving their team toward that shared vision. Leaders need to maintain their focus and constantly visualize the final product. They cannot be deterred, distracted, or derailed by insignificant details or small bumps in the road. They should always keep in mind that they do not coach against an opponent, as much has they coach against a vision of how good they think their own team can be, and then take the necessary steps to reach that goal. These coaches set challenging goals for their team daily, weekly, and for the season – goals that require everyone to stretch themselves to better the group.

Every successful team needs the direction that is provided by a clearly defined, challenging vision. It establishes a purpose to passion and allows individuals to accept complimentary roles. The clearest of visions ties together the past, present, and future of the team. Everyone who is aware of the team's vision can then say, "I know where we are going."

"But the bravest are surely those with the clearest vision of what is before them, glory and danger alike, and yet notwithstanding, go out and meet it."

— Pericles

"Dreams are free."

— Unknown

"I slept and dreamt that life was joy. I awake and saw that life was service. I acted, and behold, service was a joy."

— Rabindranath Tagore

"Vision is the art of seeing the invisible."

— Jonathan Swift

"Prophets, mystics, poets, scientific discoverers are men whose lives are dominated by a vision; they are essentially solitary men... whose thoughts and emotions are not subject to dominion of the herd."

— Bertrand Russell

"Every time an artist dies, part of the vision of mankind passes with him."

— Franklin D. Roosevelt

"Far away there in the sunshine are my highest aspirations. I may not reach them, but I can look up and see their beauty, believe in them and follow them where they lead."

— Louisa May Alcott

"If there were dreams to sell, what would you buy?"

— Thomas Lovell Beddoes

"No vision and you perish; no ideal and you're lost;
Your heart must ever cherish some faith at any cost;
Some hope, some dream to cling to; some rainbow in the sky;
Some melody to sing to; some service that is high."

— Harriet Du Autermont

"Hold fast to your dreams, for if dreams die, life is a broken winged bird that cannot fly."

— Langston Hughes

"Three levels of organizational vision:
1. The Do-able 2. The Conceivable 3. The Previously Unthinkable

— Unknown

""It is alright to aim high if you have plenty of ammunition."

— Hawley R. Everhart

We grow by dreams. All big men are dreamers. Some of us let our dreams die, but others nourish and protect them, nurse them though the bad days… to the sunshine and light which always comes."

— Woodrow Wilson

"Three people were at work on a construction site. All were doing the same job, but when asked what the job was, the answers varied. 'Breaking rocks,' the first replied. 'Earning a living,' the second said. 'Helping build a cathedral,' said the third."

— Peter Schultz

"I'll do my dreaming with my eyes wide open, and I'll do my looking back with my eyes closed."

— Tony Arata

"We need to learn to set our course by the stars, not by the lights of every passing ship."

— Omar Bradley

"Vision looks inwards and becomes duty. Vision looks outwards and becomes aspiration. Vision looks upward and becomes faith."

— Stephen S. Wise

"The most pathetic person in the world is someone who has sight but has no vision."

— Helen Keller

"A vision without a task is but a dream. A task without a vision is drudgery. A vision with a task is the hope of the world."

— Unknown

"When I dream, I am ageless."

— Elizabeth Coatsworth

"Only things the dreamers make live on. They are the eternal conquerors."

— Herbert Kaufman

"The people who shape our lives and our cultures have the ability to communicate a vision or quest or a joy or a mission."

— Anthony Robbins

"Do not follow where the path may lead. Go, instead, where there is no path and leave a trail."

— Unknown

"We need to give ourselves permission to act out our dreams and visions, not look for more sensations, more phenomena, but live our strongest dreams – even if it takes a lifetime."

— Vijali Hamilton

"I have heard it said that the first ingredient of success – the earliest spark in the dreaming of youth – if this; dream a great dream."

— John A. Appleman

"Dreams are renewable. No matter what our age or condition, there are still untapped possibilities within us and new beauty waiting to be born."

— Dale Turner

"Now, I say to you today my friends, even though we face the difficulties of today and tomorrow, I still have a dream. It is a dream deeply rooted in the American dream. I have a dream that one day this nation will rise up and live out the true meaning of its creed: we hold these truths to be self-evident, that all men are created equal."

— Martin Luther King Jr.

"When your heart is in your dream, no request is too extreme."

— Jiminy Cricket

"If you would hit the mark, you must aim a little above it;
Every arrow that flies feels the attraction of the earth."

— Henry Wadsworth Longfellow

"How far is far, and how high is high? We'll never know until we try."

— Song from the
California Special Olympics

"Nothing is as real as a dream. The world can change around you, but your dream will not. Responsibilities need not erase it. Duties need not obscure it. Because the dream is within you, no one can take it away."

— Tom Clancy

"Dream no small dreams for they have no power to move the hearts of men."

— Goethe

"I am neither an optimist nor a pessimist, but a possibilist."

— Max Learner

"Build it and they will come."

— Field of Dreams

"...daydreams, as it were...I look out the window sometimes to seek the color of the shadows and the different greens in the trees, but when I get ready to paint I just close my eyes and imagine a scene."

— "Grandma" Moses

"A dream is a microscope through which we look at the hidden occurrences in our soul."

— Erich Fromm

"Certainly a leader needs a clear vision of the organization and where it is going, but a vision is of little value unless it is shared in a way so as to generate enthusiasm and commitment."

— Claude Taylor

"If a little dreaming is dangerous, the cure for it is not to dream less but to dream more, to dream all the time."

— Marcel Proust

"Dreams are...illustrations from the book your soul is writing about you."

— Marsha Norman

"Greatness is the dream of youth realized in old age."

— Alfred Victor Vigny

"Dreams say what they mean, but they don't say it in daytime language."

— Gail Godwin

I Teach...

"I speak from my heart.
They speak from the lives.

I listen to hear them with my heart.
They listen with theirs.

I read to brighten my life.
They read to broaden theirs.

I write to show them meaning.
They write to show me they understand.

I watch as they grow and am happy.
They watch themselves grow and feel pride.

I share to allow an exchange.
They share to find a piece for themselves.

I care because they belong to me.
They care because we belong to each other.

I teach because I dream.
They learn because they dream also.

— Julie Yantz-Foley

"I have had dreams, and I've had nightmares.
I overcame the nightmares because of my dreams."

— Jonas Salk

"I was not looking for my dreams to interpret my life,
but rather for my life to interpret my dreams."

— Susan Sontag

"The poor man is not he who is without a cent, but he who is without a dream."
— Harry Kemp

"We must teach our children to dream with their eyes open."
— Harry Edwards

"Let them grow, but guide them.
Let them grow, but support their dreams.
Let them grow, but allow them to fail.
Let them grow, but offer them wisdom.
Let them grow, but accept them where they are.
Let them grow, but teach them values.
Let them grow, but don't mold them.
Let them grow, but show them discipline.
Let them grow, but model responsibility.
Let them grow, and unconditionally love them."
— Ann S. Morris

MOTIVATE WITH YOUR HEART AND PASSION

"Heart separates the good from the great."
— Michael Jordan

Heart is the energy center of the team and it ignites commitment. No external motivators can function or influence as powerfully as the well-constructed heart of a team. Some leaders have a personal make up that contains deeper feeling and a fire inside them that others do not experience. They are passionate about what they do and have the ability to spread that passion to team members who may never be able to sense it or initiate it themselves. Passion lights the path to accomplishment.

The heart of a passionate leader is shared throughout the team with words, action, and by example. Each player's heart reflects the true inner person and it cannot be disguised or ignored. Sometimes passions are seen in explosions of individual emotions and, at other times, in the fire of enthusiasm that is spread to the entire team. More often than not, a team of low ability that prepares and performs with great passion can defeat a talented team that is without passion.

Regardless of how passion is displayed, it is capable of inspiration. Passion strengthens the will of everyone connected to the team and allows possibilities where none appeared to previously exist. When teams lose their passion, practice becomes work, and sacrifice becomes a hardship. Teams are often able to develop an identity of their own, but more often than not, they will let the heart of the leader be their guide. As such, passionate leaders have to discover a method to actively evoke the positive potential present in the hearts of others so that energy is shared, direction is clearly established, and the group develops the strength of a collective heartbeat.

"Passions are vices or virtues to the highest powers.

— Goethe

"Not the glittering weapon fights the fight, but rather the hero's heart."

— Proverb

"There are many paths to enlightenment. Be sure to take the one with a heart."

— Lao Tzu

"Passion doesn't look beyond the moment for its existence."

— Christian Nevell Bovee

"You can pursue happiness by wearing a torn jersey.
You can catch it by being good at something you love."

— George Will

"Passion costs me too much to bestow it on every trifle."

— Thomas Adams

"We could hardly wait to get up in the morning."

— Wilbur Wright

"We must act our passion before we can feel it."

— Jean Paul Sartre

"Honest criticism means nothing; what one wants is unrestrained passion, fire for fire."

— Henry Miller

"Let your heart guide you. It whispers, so listen closely."
— The Land Before Time

"The more extreme and the more expressed the passion is,
the more unbearable does life seem without it."
— John Boorman

"You can buy a person's hand, but you can't buy their heart.
His heart is where his enthusiasm, his loyalty is."
— Steven Covey

"Within your heart, keep one still, secret spot where dreams may go."
— Louise Driscoll

"Doubt obscures the true vision of the heart."
— Unknown

"When we know to read our own hearts, we acquire wisdom of the hearts of others."
— Denis Diderot

"God has placed the world in man's heart."
— Solomon

"Follow your heart, but be quiet for a while first. Ask questions, then feel the answer.
Learn to trust your heart."
— Unknown

"Some people carry their heart in their head and some carry their head in their heart.
The trick is to keep them apart yet working together."
— David Hare

"Light breaks where no sun shines; Where no sea runs,
the waters of the heart push their tides."
— Dylan Thomas

"Where your treasure is, there will your heart be also."

— Matthew 6:21

"To a young heart, everything is fun."

— Charles Dickens

"When God measures a man, he puts a tape around his heart, not his head."

— Guideposts

"The prudence of the best heads is often defeated by tenderness of the best hearts."

— Henry Fielding

"If I keep a green bough in my heart, the singing bird will come."

— Chinese Proverb

"We live in deeds, not years; in thoughts, not breaths;
In feelings, not figures on a dial.
We should count time by heart throbs.
He most lives, who thinks most, feels the noblest, acts the best."

— Festus Bailey

"The human body can do so much and then the heart and spirit take over."

— Sung Ki Chung,
Olympic marathon winner

"A royal heart is often hidden under a tattered cloak."

— Danish Proverb

"A friend is the hope of the heart."

— Ralph Waldo Emerson

"Some people, no matter how old they get, never lose their beauty - - they simply move it from their faces into their hearts."

— Martin Buxbaum

"Happiness, like a refreshing stream, flows from heart to heart in endless circulation."

— Henry Grove

"The great man is he who does not lose his child's heart."

— Mencius

"Hot heads and cold hearts never solved a problem."

— Billy Graham

"Hearts are strongest when they beat in response to noble ideals."

— Ralph Bunche

"There are many who had rather meet their bitterest enemy
in the field than their own hearts in their closet."

— Charles Caleb Colton

CHAPTER 6

Persistence

- Challenges
- Courage
- Mistakes

GREAT TEAMS HAVE PERSISTENCE

"The gem cannot be polished without friction, nor the person without trials."
— Unknown

Adversity is a good thing for young people to experience. Winning all the time can mask unresolved issues and give young people an unrealistic view of life. Athletics is one of the best areas in a young person's life to go through difficult times. Few failures in athletics do permanent damage or have life-long implications. There is almost always another practice or game, and good teams have a built-in support system.

There will never be any such thing as a perfect season, perfect game or even a perfect practice session. Problems will always arise. Problems with winning and losing, injuries, relationships, etc. will emerge when they are least expected. Great teams can endure through the difficulties, which come during any athletic season. On great teams, when a problem exists, they solve it. All failures and problems need to be examined and dealt with directly. Methods should be devised with the goal of eliminating the reoccurrence of that particular problem. These teams also understand that it takes time to reach their potential individually and even longer collectively. Great teams have no quit in them.

The ability for both teams and individuals to recover quickly from mistakes is one of the keys to success. Players who dwell on mistakes tend to compound them. If a team has committed itself to continuous improvement, it must risk failure. Many times, games are just a series of mistakes, and it is the team that recovers the quickest from these mistakes that most often wins.

"You win some, you lose some, some get rained out, but you gotta suit up for them all."
— J. Askenberg

"My barn has burned to the ground, I can now see the moon.
— Taoist saying

"I can accept failure, everyone fails at something. But I can't accept not trying."
— Michael Jordan

"Pray not for a lighter load, but for stronger shoulders."
— Unknown

"The first time you quit, it's hard. The second time, it gets easier.
The third time, you don't even have to think about it."

— Paul "Bear" Bryant

"We could never learn to be brave and patient if there were only joy in the world."

— Helen Keller

"Adversity has the same effect on a man that severe training has on a pugilist, it reduces him to fighting weight."

— Josh Billings

"One often learns more from ten days of agony than from ten years of contentment."

— Merle Shain

"Life has meaning only in the struggle. Triumph or defeat is in the hands of the Gods. So let us celebrate the struggle."

— Swahili Warrior Song

"Gray skies are just clouds passing over."

— Duke Ellington

"Life is not easy for any of us. We must have perseverance an above all confidence in ourselves. We must believe that we are gifted for something and this thing must be attained."

— Marie Curie

"If we study the lives of great men and women carefully and unemotionally we find that, invariably, greatness was developed, tested and revealed through the darker periods of their lives. One of the largest tributaries of the River of Greatness is always the Stream of Adversity."

— Cavett Robert

"Perseverance is a great element of success; if you only knock long enough and loud enough at the gate, you are sure to wake up somebody."

— Henry Wadsworth Longfellow

"God will not look you over for medals, degrees, or diplomas, but for scars."
— Elbert Hubbard

"What appears to be calamities are often the sources of fortune."
— Benjamin Disraeli

"Every silver lining has a cloud."
— Avon

"If you aren't in over your head, how do you know how tall you are."
— Unknown

"There is in every woman's heart a spark of heavenly fires, which lies dormant in the broad daylight of prosperity; but which kindles up, and beams and blazes in the dark hour of adversity."
— Washington Irving

"Perseverance is not a long race; it is many short races one after another."
— Walter Elliott

"Be not elated by fortune, be not depressed by adversity."
— Cleobulus

"It's not that I'm so smart, it's just that I stay with problems longer."
— Albert Einstein

"Little drops of water wear down big stones."
— Russian Proverb

"I have always tried to teach my players to be fighters. When I say that, I don't mean put up your dukes and get in a fistfight over something. I'm talking about facing adversity in your life. There is not a person alive who isn't going to have some awfully bad days in the their lives."
— Paul "Bear" Bryant

"The bravest sight in the world is to see a great man struggling against adversity."

— Seneca

"In dark times, the eye begins to see."

— Theodore Roethke

"We must free ourselves of the hope that the seas will ever rest.
We must learn to sail in high winds."

— Hanmer Parsons Grant

"My greatest point is my persistence. I never give up in a match. However down I am, I fight until the last ball. My matches show that I have turned a great many so-called irretrievable defeats into victories."

— Bjorn Borg

"There could be no honor in a sure success,
but much might be wrested from a sure defeat."

— Thomas E. Lawrence

"What has passed and cannot be prevented, should not be grieved for."

— Big Elk, Maha Chief

"Every blade of grass has its angel that bends over it and whispers, 'Grow, grow.'"

— The Talmud

"Difficulty is the nurse of greatness, a harsh nurse, who roughly rocks her foster children into strength and athletic proportion."

— William C. Bryant

"Adversity is the state in which man most easily becomes acquainted with himself, being especially free of admirers.

— Samuel Johnson

"Pain is inevitable, suffering is optional."

— M. Kathleen Casey

"It is easy enough to be pleasant, when life flows like a song.
But the man worthwhile is the one who can smile, when everything goes dead wrong.
For the test of the heart is troubled, and it always comes with years,
And the smiles that is worth the praises of earth is the smile that shines though the tears."

— Ella Wheeler Wilcox

"Fire is the test of gold, adversity, of strong men.

— Seneca

"What is to give light must endure burning."

— Victor E. Frankl

"In the depth of winter, I finally learned that within me there lay an invincible summer."

— Albert Camus

"If your knees are knocking, kneel on them."

— Unknown

"Turn your face to the sun and the shadows fall behind you."

— Maori Proverb

"Some people bear three kinds of trouble; the ones they've had; the ones the have; and the ones they expect to have."

— Edward Everett Hale

"People are like stained-glass windows. They sparkle and shine when the sun is out, but when the darkness sets in, their true beauty is revealed only if there is a light from within."

— Elizabeth Kubler Ross

"Two frogs fell into a bowl of cream. One didn't panic, he relaxed and drowned. The other kicked and struggled so much that the cream turned to butter and he walked out."

— Unknown

"You become a champion by fighting one more round.
When things are tough, you fight one more round."

— James J. Corbett

"You never know what events are going to transpire to get you home."

— Apollo 13 Movie

"Life is truly known only to those who suffer, lose, endure adversity
and stumble from defeat to defeat."

— Ryszard Kapuscinski

"It is not for all our wishes to be filled; through sickness we recognize the value
of health; through evil, the value of good; through hunger, the value of food;
through exertion, the value of rest.

— Greek saying

"Persistence is to the character of man as carbon is to steel."

— Napoleon Hill

"If I had a formula for bypassing trouble, I would not pass it around. Trouble creates a
capacity to handle it. I don't embrace trouble; that is as bad as treating it as an
enemy. But I do say meet it as a friend, for you'll see a lot of it and you had better
be on speaking terms with it."

— Oliver Wendell Holmes

"In prosperity our friends know us; in adversity, we know our friends."

— John Churton Collins

"Sometimes your medicine bottle has on it, 'shake well before using.'
That is what God has to do with some of His people. He has to shake them
well before they are ever usable."

— Vance Havner

"It is not so important who starts the game but who finishes it."

— John Wooden

"Persevere in virtue and diligence."

— Titus Livy

"The willow which bends to the tempest, often escapes better than the oak which resists it."

— Sir Walter Scott

"It takes a real storm in the average person's life to make him realize how much worrying he has done over squalls."

— Heartland Advisor

"A reasonable amount of fleas is good for a dog, it keeps him form brooding over being a dog."

— Edward Noyes Westcott

"No pressure, no diamonds."

— Mary Case

"Never let your head hang down. Never give up and sit down and grieve. Find another way. And don't pray when it rains if you don't pray when the sun shines."

— Leroy Satchel Paige

"For a righteous man falls seven times and rises again."

— Proverbs 24:16

PERSIST TO OVERCOME CHALLENGES

"Accept the challenge so that you may feel the exhilaration of victory."

— George S. Patton

As the challenges grow larger, the need for teamwork elevates. Some challenges are unexpected, and individuals have no choice but to take them head on. Some challenges are dreams that individuals create and then try to meet. For anything great to happen, it takes people to dream and follow their heart. In this regard one of the best exercises for anyone to undertake is to write down a list of one hundred things that they want to accomplish during their life, and then start checking them off. When good teams have big dreams, their potential is tested, and the challenges of achieving those dreams become a shared experience that bonds them. When bad teams have big dreams, their weaknesses are exposed—and their dreams turn into nightmares. A team and its dreams must have matching strengths. Overcoming difficult challenges is one of the best methods to develop the "shared joy of the inner circle" kind of pride and building teams.

"It is surmounting difficulties that makes heroes."

— Louis Kossuth

"Mountains cannot be surmounted except by winding paths."

— Goethe

"Hardship and opposition are the native soil of manhood and self-reliance."

— John Neil

"In the final analysis, the questions of why bad things happen to good people transmutes itself into some very different questions, no longer asking why something happened, but asking how we will respond, what we intend to do now that it happened."

— Rabbi Harold S. Kushner

"All things are difficult before they are easy."

— John Norley

"Never look down to test the ground before taking your next step, only he who keeps his eyes fixed on the far horizon will find his right road."

— Dag Hammarskjold

When Dr. David Livingstone was on a mission to Africa another missionary organization wanted to send assistance to him and they wrote, "Have you found a good road to where you are? If so, we want to send other men to join you." Livingstone replied, "If you have men who will come only if they know there is a good road, I don't want them. I want men who will come if there is no road at all."

"I know God will not give me anything I can't handle.
I just wish that He didn't trust me so much."

— Mother Teresa

"It isn't the mountain ahead that wears you out; it's the grain of sand in your shoe."

— Robert W. Service

"There's no thrill in easy sailing when the skies are clear and blue,
there's no joy in merely doing things which anyone can do.
But there is some satisfaction that is mighty sweet to take,
when you reach a destination that you thought you'd never reach."

— Spirella

"Obstacles are like wild animals. They are cowards but they will bluff you if they can.
If they see you are afraid of them, they are liable to spring upon you,
if you look them squarely in the eye, they will slink out of sight."

— Orison Swett Marden

"Difficulties strengthen the mind, as labor does the body."

— Seneca

"Adventure is not hanging on a rope off the side of a mountain. Adventure is an attitude that we must apply to the day to day obstacles of life – facing new challenges, seizing new opportunities, testing our resources against the unknown and in the process, discovering our own unique potential."

— John Armitt

"Life is a constant oscillation between the sharp horns of dilemmas."

— H.L. Mencken

"You can lay down and die, or you can get up and fight, but that is it – there is no turning back."

— Jon English

PERSISTENCE REQUIRES COURAGE

"With courage you will dare to take risks, have the strength to be compassionate and the wisdom to be humble. Courage is the foundation of integrity."

— Keshavan Nair

Courage can be found in large or small actions, based on principles rather than perceptions. Although displays of courage do not require a crisis, adversity makes courage extremely visible. Most of individuals have far more courage than they give themselves credit for. It requires courage for individuals to submit themselves to the betterment of the team, to accept a role and perform duties with excellence, to develop a sense of duty to each other regardless of the circumstances. The main form of courage required for successful teams is the ability to act on and live out the guiding principles underlying the team and to become dependable, teammates with integrity. Having the courage to consistently and persistently adhere to appropriate values gives authenticity and positive power to the team. When a team visualizes courage in this way, it is contagious. A team will grow in all directions in direct proportion to its courage.

"Live as brave men and face adversity with stout hearts."

— Horace

"The ultimate measure of a man is not where he stands in moments of comfort and convenience, but where he stands at times of challenge and controversy."

— Martin Luther King Jr.

"Stand upright, speak thy thoughts, declare the truth thou hast, that all may share; Be bold, proclaim it everywhere: They only live who dare."

— Lewis Morris

"Cowards can never be moral."

— Mahatma Ghandi

"Life shrinks or expands in proportion to one's courage."

— Anais Nin

"Wisdom and courage make mutual contributions to greatness."

— Baltasar Gracian

"Like a boxer in a title fight, you have to walk in that ring alone."

— Billy Joel

"It is not because things are difficult that we do not dare; it is because we do not dare that they are difficult."

— Seneca

"When a brave man takes a stand, the spines of others are stiffened."

— Billy Graham

"Finite to fail, but infinite to venture."

— Emily Dickinson

"What might be a brave choice for you, for another person they may simply not experience fear."

— Marlon Brando

"Relaxation frees the heart. Courage opens the heart. Compassion fills the heart."

— Kall

"If we have courage and tenacity of our forebearers, who stood firmly like a rock against the lash of slavery, we shall find a way to do for our day what they did for theirs."

— Mary Mcleod Bethune

"Act boldly and unseen forces will come to your aid."

— Dorothea Brande

"The pressure of adversity does not affect the mind of the brave man. It is more powerful than external circumstances."

— Seneca

"Without courage, wisdom bears no fruit."

— Baltasar Bracian

"Have courage for the great sorrows of life, and patience for the small ones. When you have laboriously accomplished your daily tasks, go to sleep in peace, God is awake."

— Victor Hugo

"Courage is not the towering oak that sees the storms come and go; it is the fragile blossom that opens in the snow."

— Alice Mackenzie Swaim

"Fear not that your life will come to an end, but that it will never have a beginning."

— John Henry Newman

"Real heroes are men who fall and fail and flawed, but win out in the end because they've stayed true to their ideals and beliefs and commitments."

— Kevin Costner

"Courage is fire, and bullying is smoke."

— Benjamin Disraeli

"The future does not belong to those who are content with today, apathetic toward common problems and their fellow man alike, timid and fearful in the face of bold projects and new ideas. Rather, it will belong to those who can blend passion, reason and courage in a personal commitment to the ideals of American society."

— Robert F. Kennedy

"The scars you acquire while exercising courage will never make you feel inferior."

— D. A. Battista

"True courage is cool and calm. The bravest men have the least of brutal, bullying insolence, and in the very time of danger are found the most serene and free."

— Lord Shaftesbury

"We must build dikes of courage to hold back the flood of fear."

— Martin Luther King Jr.

"Bravery is the capacity to perform properly even when scared half to death."

— Omar Bradley

"Only those who dare to fail greatly can ever achieve greatly."

— Robert F. Kennedy

"A man is a hero, not because he is braver than anyone else,
but because he is brave for ten minutes longer."

— Ralph Waldo Emerson

"Is he alone who has courage on his right hand and faith on his left hand?"

— Charles A. Lindbergh

"Courage is fear that has said its prayers."

— Dorothy Bernard

"Self-control is only courage under another form. It may also be regarded as the primary essence of character."

— Samuel Smiles

"A great deal of talent is lost to the world for want of a little courage."

— Goethe

"Perfect courage consists in doing that without witnesses, which it would be capable of doing before all the world."

— LaRochefoucauld

"The test of tolerance comes when we are in a majority; the test of courage comes when we are in a minority."

— Ralph W. Stockman

"Heroism is the brilliant triumph of the soul over the flesh, over fear. Heroism is the dazzling and glorious concentration of courage."

— Henri-Frederic Amiel

"Rest not. Life is sweeping by; go and dare before you die. Something mighty and sublime, leave behind to conquer time."

— Goethe

"Heroes are people who rise to the occasion and slip away quietly."

— Tom Brokaw

"And what he greatly thought, he nobly dared."

— Homer

"Courage faces fear and thereby masters it."

— Martin Luther King Jr.

"The brave don't live forever, but the cautious don't live at all. Here's to the brave!"

— Timothy Luce

"In fear, the brain starves the heart of its bravest blood."

— Kall

MISTAKES AND PERSISTENCE

"No man fails who does his best."

— Orison Swett Marden

Making mistakes are a basic requirement for progress and essential for learning to take place. Athletes afraid of making mistakes become stagnant and fail to improve. A team that plays in fear of making mistakes plays timidly. The best of teams play with a fearlessness that defines them. Teams that can compete with a fearless personality are difficult to defeat; they can always come back, they never give up, and they feel like they fear no opponent or situation. Fearless play is a sign of respect and trust for the coach and for each other.

Having coaches and teammates who understand and accept the fact that making mistakes is a meaningful part of the process of getting better is an essential element for everyone gaining full benefit from that process. This factor is what develops a fearless personality. Players understand that making mistakes is the only path to improvement, and they trust each other enough to approach all mistakes made with complete concentration and effort, thereby freeing themselves to make mistakes, recover quickly, and pick each other up.

"Nobody makes a greater mistake than he who does nothing because he could only do a little."

— Edmund Burke

"If I had my life to live again. I'd make the same mistakes, only sooner."

— Tallulah Bankhead

Victory goes to the player who makes the next-to-the-last mistake."

— Tartalcouen

"So go ahead and make mistakes. Make all you can, because that's where you will find success. On the far side of failure."

— Thomas J. Watson

"In order to succeed, your desire for success should be greater than your fear of failure."

— Bill Cosby

"You build on failure. You use it as a stepping stone. Close the door on the past. You don't try to forget the mistakes, but don't dwell on them. You don't let it have any of your energy, or any of your time, or any of your space."

— Johnny Cash

"It's discouraging to make a mistake, but it's humiliation when you find out you're so unimportant nobody noticed it."

— Chuck Daly

"Mistakes are a fact of life. It is the response to error that counts."

— Nikki Giovanni

"The way to succeed is to double your failure rate."

— Thomas J. Watson

"I am positive that a doer makes mistakes."

— John Wooden

"To avoid criticism, do nothing, say nothing, be nothing."

— Elbert Hubbard

"There are two mistakes one can make along the road to truth – not going all the way, and not starting."

— Buddha

"You must learn from the mistakes of others. You can't possibly live long enough to make them all yourself."

— Sam Levenson

"The greatest blunders, like the thickest ropes are often compounded of a multitude of strands. Take the rope apart, separate it into the small threads that compose it, and you can break them one by one. You think, 'that is all there was!' But twist them all together and you get something tremendous."

— Victor Hugo

"It is an unequalled gift to be able to squeeze big mistakes into small opportunities."

— Henry James

"Half our mistake in life arise from feeling where we ought to think, and thinking where we ought to feel."

— John Churton Collins

"There is glory in a great mistake."

— Nathalia Crane

"I must tell you, I take terrible risks. Because my playing is very clear, when I make a mistake you hear it. Never be afraid to dare."

— Vladimir Horowitz

"Many times the best way, in fact the only way, to learn is though mistakes. A fear of making mistakes can bring individuals to a standstill, to a dead center. Fear is the wicked wand that transforms human beings into vegetables."

— George Brown

"More people would learn from their mistakes if they weren't so busy denying them."

— Harold J. Smith

"Nowadays most people die of a sort of creeping common sense, and discover when it is too late that the only things one never regrets are one's mistakes."

— Oscar Wilde

"Losing doesn't make me want to quit. It makes me want to fight that much harder."

— Paul "Bear" Bryant

A few years ago, at the Seattle Special Olympics, nine contestants all physically or mentally disabled, assembled at the starting line for the 100-meter dash. At the gun, they all started out, not exactly in a dash, but with a relish to run the race to the finish and win. All, that is, except for one little boy who stumbled on the asphalt, tumbled over a couple of times, and began to cry. The other eight heard the boy cry. They slowed down and looked back. Then they all turned around and went back. Every one of them.

One girl with Down's Syndrome bent down and kissed him and said: "This will make it better." Then all nine linked arms and walked together to the finish line. Everyone in the stadium stood, and the cheering went on for several minutes. People who were there are still telling the story. Why? Because deep down we know this one thing: What matters in this life is more than winning for ourselves. What matters in this life is helping others win, even if it means slowing down and changing our course.

CHAPTER 7

Positive Attitude

- Behavior
- Opportunities and Choices
- Success, Achievement, and Excellence

GREAT TEAMS HAVE A POSITIVE ATTITUDE

"One of the illusions of life is that the present hour is not the critical, decisive hour. Write it on your heart that every day is the best day of the year."

– Ralph Waldo Emerson

The final quality of great teams is for everyone involved with the group to have a positive attitude and belief about the game, the team, and themselves. Attitude is a choice, but often one that has to be taught and molded. Good attitudes can be taught. As such, players can be held accountable for those attitudes that they hold. Coaches should identify and define what a positive attitude looks like in their program as specifically as possible. The clearer the description, the more likely their players will understand and be able to meet whatever standards their coach sets. Teams are very much like any other relationship; they must be constantly worked at in order to function well. The attitude of a team is the clearest reflection of the leadership of that team.

The following definition can be used as a benchmark of what an athletic attitude should involve: *Be aggressive, disciplined and love to compete. Be intelligent enough to listen and develop the self-motivation to work hard and learn. Have faith in the people you are working with and always put the team ahead of yourself. Keep your perspective and sense of humor.* At this point, it then becomes important to define each of these areas (aggressive, disciplined, loving to compete etc.) so that all team members and coaches are on the exact same page.

As a rule, attitudes are much more within the coach's control than the talent level of his athletes and, therefore, should be an area of particular focus when the coach is choosing his team. As such, having a positive athletic attitude can and should be used as one of the main criteria for squad selection. If a coach is able to establish a base standard concerning what is and is not acceptable with regard to player attitudes and strictly adhere to this standard when selecting the squad as the "line in the sand," it will help everyone involved on the team. For the player who needs to make changes, the coach should begin working with him long before the season begins, and do everything in his power to assist in creating the necessary changes. That player will be helped by knowing well ahead of time exactly what is going to be accepted and what behaviors will not. In this regard, no surprises should occur for either party by the time tryouts begin.

Once specific standards of behavior have been established and held to, the individuals who are sincerely interested in making the team will know and make their own personal choices regarding their attitude. As a consequence, the coach will have very few, if any, cuts based on attitude. Once this factor has become tradition and very clear to potential team members, the coach will discover that maintaining a great team attitude is much easier than the work it took to build it. Having an athletic attitude should be one of the most important factors for determining who is chosen to be a part of the team. Players who have a great athletic attitude deserve to have teammates who are as committed, disciplined, hard-working, and coachable as they are.

"Coaches have a tendency to stay too long with people with 'potential'. Try to avoid those players and go with a proven attitude. Players who live on 'potential' are coach killers. As soon as you find out who the coach killers are on your team, the better off you are. Go with the guys who have less talent but more dedication, more singleness of purpose."

— Don Shula

Talent alone will only take a team so far. The combination of ability plus attitude is what allows a team to enjoy the experience of reaching its potential. Attitude and potential for success are directly proportional to each other. Successful coaches surround themselves with positive, energetic people who share their passion for life, sport and team. On the other hand, negativism is contagious and undermines the motives, strategies, and covenants of the team. Coaches should be optimists who accentuates the positive—their team needs it from them. Positive attitude is a choice every person can make on a daily basis. In this regard, everything is how a person *chooses* to see it. Individuals should look harder for the good in every situation and person. Coaches should generously reaffirm, endorse, and praise the character traits over which their team has complete control – effort, attitude and virtue.

"You cannot be healthy; You cannot be happy;
You cannot be prosperous; If you have a bad disposition."

— Emmet Fox

"I think the most important thing of all for any team is a winning attitude.
The coaches must have it. The players must have it. The student body must have it.
If you have dedicated players who believe in themselves, you don't need a lot of talent."

— Paul "Bear" Bryant

"I became and optimist when I discovered that I wasn't going to win any more games by being anything else."

— Earl Weaver

Ken bought a bat and a ball for his six-year-old son who immediately ran out to the yard to practice. He threw the ball in the air and swung and at it over and over. After about an hour, he came to his father and said, "Dad, come watch how good I am."

The boy threw the ball up and took a mighty swing, and missed. "Strike one," he yelled enthusiastically. He threw the ball again and missed again. "Strike two," he called out. Ken said, "concentrate son, remember, three strikes and you're out." The boy bit his lip, threw the ball high in the air and took a terrific swing, hitting nothing but air. Ken winced but the boy looked triumphant. "Son, you struck out. Why are you so happy?" "Cause I'm proud of how good I got at pitching." And Ken's anxiety about his son melted into delight.

What an excellent example of the power of attitude. This isn't just a question of looking at the glass and saying it's half empty or half full. The boy was thrilled simply to have a glass. Because of his great attitude he could have fun and feel good even about striking himself out.

What is more, his positive attitude not only affected his own sense of happiness, but it created joy for his father. Attitudes are contagious. While cynical and sour people bring us down, cheerful, optimistic and upbeat people lift us up.

"Love is sunshine, hate is shadow. Life is checkered shade and sunshine."

— Henry Wadsworth Longfellow

"Ability is what you are capable of doing. Motivation determines what you do. Attitude determines how well you do it."

— Lou Holtz

"Life is a coin. You can spend it any way you wish, but you can only spend it once."

— Lillian Dickson

"If you are going to achieve excellence in big things, you develop the habit in little matters. Excellence is not an exception, it is a prevailing attitude."

— Colin Powell

"May you live all the days of your life."

— Jonathan Swift

"My mother taught me very early to believe I could achieve any accomplishment I wanted to. The first was to walk without braces."

— Wilma Rudolph

"When it comes to attitude and effort, coaches should demand in direct proportion to the love they have for their athletes and for the game."

— Eamon Brown

"If you smile when no one else is around, you really mean it."

— Andy Rooney

"For every minute you are angry, you lose sixty seconds of happiness."

— Ralph Waldo Emerson

"Instead of complaining, contribute."

— Unknown

"If they don't have a winning attitude, I don't want them."

— Paul "Bear " Bryant

"Each day, be sure to laugh, to think, to cry; that is one heckuva day."

— Jim Valvano

"Keep your face to the sunshine and you cannot see the shadow."

— Helen Keller

"Life is too short to spend your precious time trying to convince a person who wants to live in gloom and doom otherwise. Give lifting that person your best shot, but don't hang around long enough for his or her bad attitude to pull you down. Instead, surround yourself with optimistic people."

— Zig Ziglar

"To the world you might be one person, but to one person you might be the world."

— Unknown

"Before I was enlightened, I chopped wood and carried water.
After I became enlightened, I chopped wood and carried water."

— Zen Teaching

"Lives that flash in sunshine, and lives that are born in tears,
receive their hue from circumstance."

— Harriet A. Jacobs

"I have a good hearty laugh and energetic handshake, and those are trump cards."

— Albert Camus

"The optimist see opportunity in every danger,
the pessimist sees danger in every opportunity."

— Winston Churchill

"If you don't like something, change it. If you can't change it, change your attitude.
Don't complain."

— Maya Angelou

"A strong positive attitude will create more miracles than any wonder drug."

— Patricia Neal

"What sunshine is to flowers, smiles are to humanity. There are but trifles, to be sure;
but, scattered along life's pathway, the good they do is inconceivable."

— Joseph Addison

"The winner asks, 'May I help?' The loser asks, 'Do you expect me to do that?'"

— William Arthur Ward

"We must learn to reawaken and keep ourselves awake."

— Thoreau

"Deal with the faults of others as gently as with your own."

— Chinese Proverb

"You can complain because the roses have thorns, or you can rejoice because the thorns have roses."

— Ziggy

"There is little difference in people, but that little difference is attitude. The big difference is whether it is positive or negative."

— W. Clement Stone

"I had no shoes and complained until I met a man who had no feet."

— Indian Proverb

"If wrinkles must be written upon our brows, let them not be written upon the heart. The spirit should never grow old."

— Abraham Lincoln

"Weakness of attitude becomes weakness of character."

— Albert Einstein

"Seek out that particular mental attribute which makes you feel most deeply and vitally alive, along with which comes the inner voice which says, 'This is the real me' and when you have found that attitude, follow it."

— James Truslow Adams

"What fire could equal the sunshine of a winter's day?"

— Henry David Thoreau

"The last of the human freedoms – to choose one's attitude in any given set of circumstances, to choose one's own way."

— Dr. Viktor E. Fankl

"Happiness is like a pair of eyeglasses correcting your spiritual vision."

— Lloyd Morris

"The best way to predict your future is to create it."

— Unknown

"Inspire and motivate your players with praise. Ten years from now, it won't matter what your record was. Will your kids love you or hate you?"

— Jim Harrick

"The remarkable thing we have is a choice every day regarding the attitude we will embrace for that day. We cannot change our past...We cannot change the fact that people will act in a certain way. We cannot change the inevitable. The only thing we can do is play on the one string we have, and that is our attitude."

— Charles Swindoll

"Body and spirit are twins; God only knows which is which."

— Swinburne

"I never criticize a player until they are first convinced of my unconditional confidence in their abilities."

— John Robinson

"Don't lose hope; when it gets darkest, the stars come out."

— Unknown

POSITIVE ATTITUDE IS REFLECTED BY BEHAVIOR

"Behavior is a mirror in which every one displays his image."

— Goethe

Behavior demonstrates and attaches priorities to an individual's beliefs. It validates a person's values through action. Coaches should let their behaviors speak for themselves and for their team. Individuals cannot hide who they are when they perform with others in an athletic arena. Coaches and players should let their actions and behavioral choices create their image. When people see a team play and then read the team's mission statement, are the various aspects of that directive believable?

"A false friend and a shadow attend only while the sun shines."

— Benjamin Franklin

"You are in charge of our feelings, beliefs and actions. And you teach others how to behave toward you. While you cannot change other people, you can influence them though your own behaviors and actions. By being a living role model of what you want to receive from others, you create more of what you want in your life."

— Eric Allenbaugh

"One can never consent to creep when one feels an impulse to soar."

— Helen Keller

"I once complained to my father that I didn't seem to be able to do things the same way the other people did. Dad's advice? 'Margo, don't be a sheep. People hate sheep. They eat sheep.'"

— Margo Kaufman

"To know what people really think, pay regard to what they do, rather than what they say."

— Rene Descartes

"Positiveness is a good quality for preachers and speakers because, whoever shares his thoughts with the pubic will convince them as he himself appears convinced."

— Jonathan Swift

"Feel the feeling. Choose the behavior."

— Charles Rumberg

"The American people never carry an umbrella, they prepare to walk in eternal sunshine."

— Alfred E. Smith

"The thing always happens that you believe in, and the belief in a thing, makes it happen."

— Frank Lloyd Wright

"Be an optimist – at least until they start moving animals in pairs to Cape Canaveral."

— Unknown

"The longer I live, the more I realize the impact of attitude on life. Attitude, to me is more important than facts. It is more important than the past, than education, than money, than circumstances, than failures, than successes, than what other people think or say or do. It is more important than appearance, giftedness, or skill. It will make or break a company…a church…a home. The remarkable thing is we have a choice every day regarding the attitude we will embrace for that day. I am convinced that life is 10% what happens to me and 90% how I react to it. And so it is with you…we are in charge of our attitudes."

— Charles Swindoll

"Sunshine is delicious, rain refreshing, wind braces up, snow is exhilarating; there is no such thing as bad weather, just different kinds of good weather."

— John Ruskin

"There are no menial jobs, only menial attitudes."

— William John Bennett

"Men go fishing all their lives without knowing that it is not fish they are after."

— Henry David Thoreau

"Whenever you are in conflict with someone, there is one factor that can make the difference between damaging your relationship and deepening it.
That factor is attitude."

— Timothy Bentley

"The best portion of a good man's life, his little, nameless, unremembered acts of kindness and of love."

— William Wordsworth

"If you wish to travel far and fast, travel light. Take off all your envies, jealousies, unforgiveness, selfishness and fears."

— Glenn Clark

"It is not the position, but the disposition."

— J.E. Dinger

"If you can react the same way to winning and losing, that's a big accomplishment. That quality is important because it stays with you the rest of your life, and there's going to be a life after tennis that's a lot bigger than your tennis life."

— Chris Evert

"It's how you deal with failure that determines how you achieve success."

— David Feherty

"I always want my players to show class, knock 'em down, pat 'em on the back, and run back to the huddle."

— Paul "Bear " Bryant

"It's not the load that breaks you , it is the way you choose to carry it."

— Lena Horne

"Success or failure depends more upon attitude than upon capacity. Successful men act as though they have accomplished or enjoyed something. Soon it becomes a reality. Act, look, feel successful, conduct yourself accordingly and you will be amazed at the positive results."

— Dupree Jordan

"Two men look out the same prison bars; one sees mud, the other stars."

— Frederick Langbridge

"Be thou the rainbow in the storms of life: the evening beam that smiles the clouds away, and tints tomorrow with prophetic ray."

— Byron

"If you will call your troubles experiences, and remember that every experience develops some latent force within you, you will grow vigorous and happy, however adverse your circumstance may seem to be."

— John Miller

"A good laugh is sunshine in a house."

— William Makepeace Thackeray

"Our attitude toward life determines life's attitude towards us."
— Earl Nightingale

"You play the hand you're dealt. I think the game is worthwhile."
— Christopher Reeve

"There are only 3 colors, 10 digits, and 7 notes;
it's what we do with them that is important."
— Ruth Ross

"Don't be against things so much as for things."
— Col. Harland Sanders

"This is the precept by which I have lived: Prepare for the worst;
expect the best; and take what comes."
— Robert Speer

"A healthy attitude is contagious but don't wait to catch it from others. Be a carrier."
— Unknown

"Between the optimist and the pessimist, the difference is droll. The optimist sees
the doughnut; and the pessimist sees the hole."
— Mclandburgh Wilson

"The only normal people are the ones you don't know very well."
— Joe Ancis

"Our natures are a lot like oil, mix us with anything else and we strive to swim on top."
— Francis Beaumont

"One joy dispels a hundred cares."
— Confucius

"Many people love in themselves what they hate in others."

— Benzel Sternan

"With a gentleman I am always a gentleman and a half,
with a fraud I try to be a fraud and a half."

— Otto Von Bismarck

"I place a high moral value on the way people behave. I find it repellent to have a lot and to behave with anything other than courtesy in the old sense of the word – politeness of the heart, gentleness of the spirit."

— Emma Thompson

"Be so strong that nothing can disturb your peace of mind. Talk health, happiness and prosperity to every person you meet. Make all your friends feel there is something special in them. Look at the sunny side of everything. Think only of the best, work only for the best, and expect only the best. Be as enthusiastic about the success of others as you are about your own. Forget the mistakes of the past and press on the greater achievements of the future. Give everyone a smile. Spend so much time improving yourself that you have no time left to criticize others. Be too big for worry and too noble for anger."

— Christian D. Larson

POSITIVE ATTITUDES PROVIDE OPPORTUNITIES AND CHOICES

"When the defining moment comes along, you only can do one of two things. Define the moment or let the moment define you."

— The movie Tin Cup

The ultimate future of individuals' lives is often determined by the small day-to-day choices made in the present. An individual's personal character evolves from making choices. Having the freedom to make choices is both a blessing and a burden. People will either be blessed or burdened by the outcome of decisions they make. Seeing these challenges as choices makes each of them an opportunity for growth.

Not all circumstances are in a person's control, but it remains a choice how an individual responds to uncontrollable situations. Understanding, embracing, and using the power of choices, provides opportunities for people to learn, work, build confidence, develop loyalty, and discover courage in themselves.

"Opportunity is missed by most people because it is dressed in overalls and looks like work."

— Thomas Edison

"There is no security on this earth, there is only opportunity."

— General Douglas MacArthur

"A man either lives life as it happens to him, meets it head-on and licks it, or turns his back on it and starts to wither away."

— Gene Roddenberry

"Man's power of choice enables him to think like an angel or a devil, a king or a slave. Whatever he chooses, the mind will create and manifest."

— Frederick Bailes

"Prepare yourself in every way you can by increasing your knowledge and adding to your experience, so that you can make the most of opportunity when it occurs."

— Mario Andretti

"We cannot tell what may happen to us in the strange medley of life. But we can decide what happens in us – how we can take it, what to do with it – and that is what really counts in the end – that is the test of living."

— Joseph Fort Newton

"It is better to be prepared for an opportunity and not have one, than to have an opportunity and not be prepared."

— Whitney Young Jr.

"Nowadays some people expect the door of opportunity to be opened with a remote control."

— M. Charles Wheeler

"Constantly choosing the lesser of two evils is still choosing evil."

— Jerry Garcia

"All my life, whenever it comes time to make a decision, I make it and forget about it."

— Harry S. Truman

"To every man there openeth a way.
The high soul climbs the high way.
And the low soul gropes the low:
And in between, on the misty flats, the rest drift to and fro.
But to every man there openeth a high way and a low,
And every man decideth the way his soul shall go."

— John Oxenham

"It is so hard when I have to, and so easy when I want to."

— Sondra Anice Barnes

"When you can't have what you choose, you choose what you have."

— Owen Wister

"It's always your next move."

— Napoleon Hill

"Choice strengthens all."

— Neal Prescot

"Choose your love, love your choice."

— Thomas S. Monson

"Don't wait for extraordinary circumstances to do good; try to use ordinary situations."

— Charles Richter

"Some men go through the forest and see no firewood."

— Irish Proverb

"You are the person who has to decide.
Whether you'll do it or toss it aside;

You are the person who makes up your mind.
Whether you'll lead or will linger behind.

Whether you'll try for the goal that's afar.
Or just be contented to stay where you are."

— Edgar A. Guest

"Opportunity dances with those who are ready on the dance floor."

— H. Jackson Brown Jr.

"When you make a choice, you activate vast human energies and resources, which otherwise go untapped. Too often people fail to focus their choices upon results and therefore their choices are ineffective. If you limit your choices only to what seems possible or reasonable, you disconnect yourself from what you truly want, and all that is left is compromise."

— Robert Fritz

"Great opportunities to help others seldom come, but small ones surround us daily."

— Sally Koch

"When we acknowledge that all of life is sacred and that each act is an act of choice and therefore sacred, then life is a sacred dance lived consciously each moment. When we live at this level, we participate in the creation of a better world."

— Scout Cloud Lee

"They who know how to employ opportunities will often find that they can create them; and what we can achieve depends less on the amount of time we possess than on the use we make of our time."

— John S. Mill

"There has never been another you. With no effort on your part you were born to be something very special and set apart. What you are going to do in appreciation of that gift is a decision only you can make."

— Dan Zadra

"There is an election going on all the time... the Lord votes for you and Satan votes against you, and you must cast the deciding vote."

— Unknown

"When written in Chinese, the word 'crisis' is composed of two characters – one represents danger, and the other represents opportunity."

— John F. Kennedy

POSITIVE ATTITUDES PROMOTE SUCCESS, ACHIEVEMENT AND EXCELLENCE

"I hope that my achievements in life shall be these – That I will have fought for what was right and fair, that I will have risked for that which mattered, that I will have given help to those who were in need and that I will have left the earth a better place for what I've done and who I've been."

— C. Hoppe

Positive attitudes are a huge gift to teammates. They help promote persistence, courage, and trust when things are not going well. They facilitate keeping the team moving toward its goals. They are essential in the drive to achieve excellence. A positive outlook toward the desire to succeed and to reach your full potential is the key that unlocks the door to personal and team excellence. Positive attitudes promote team spirit. That spirit comes from each individual sharing his positive energy and doing what he can to pursue personal excellence in order that the team can accomplish its mission.

Great teams are driven by excellence. Excellence depends more on a person's will than on individual's level of skill. In reality, excellence it is the will of the team on display.

"Let me tell you the secret that has led me to my goal.
My strength lies solely in my tenacity."

— Louis Pasteur

"He who has put a good finish to his undertaking is said to have placed a golden crown to the whole."

— Eustachius

"Nothing happens until I make it happen."
— Scott Wilson

"Trust yourself. Create the kind of self that you will be happy to live with all your life. Make the most of yourself by fanning the tiny, inner sparks of possibility into flames of achievement."
— Foster C. McClellan

"People seldom see the halting and painful steps by which the most insignificant success is achieved."
— Anne Sullivan

"Let us, then, be up and doing, with a heart for any fate;
Still achieving, still pursuing, learn to labor and to wait."
— Henry Wadsworth Longfellow

"Perfection does not exist – you can always do better and you can always grow."
— Les Brown

"If something is exceptionally well done it has embedded in it's very existence the aim of lifting the common denominator rather than catering to it."
— Edward Fischer

"What would you attempt to do if you knew you would not fail?"
— Robert Schuller

"Having one decided to achieve a certain task, achieve it at all costs of tedium and distaste. The gain in self confidence of having accomplished a tiresome labor is immense."
— Thomas A. Bennett

"Empty pockets never held anyone back.
Only empty heads and empty hearts can do that."
— Norman Vincent Peale

"To aim at excellence, our reputation, our friends and all must be ventured; to aim at the average we run no risk and provide little service."

— Oliver Goldsmith

"What we achieve inwardly will change outer reality."

— Otto Rank

"The person who wakes up and finds himself a success hasn't been asleep."

— Wilson Mizner

"We distinguish the excellent man from the common man by saying that the former is the one who makes great demands on himself and the latter who makes no demands on himself."

— Jose Ortega y Gasset

"It has always been my belief that a man should do his best, regardless of how much he receives for his services, or the number of people he may be serving or the class of people served."

— Napoleon Hill

"I'm not a good shot, but I shoot often."

— Theodore Roosevelt

"Success usually comes to those too busy to be looking for it."

— Henry David Thoreau

"There is a canyon of difference between doing your best to glorify God and doing whatever it takes to glorify yourself. The quest for excellence is a mark of maturity. The quest for power is childish."

— Max L. Lucado

"Do not be desirous of having things done quickly. Do not look at small advantages. Desire to have things done quickly prevents their being done thoroughly. Looking at small advantages prevents great affairs from being accomplished."

— Confucius

"Unless you are a member of a major league baseball team, your errors, unless they are truly spectacular, don't show up in the morning paper."

— Jane Goodsell

"Out of the strain of doing and into the peace of done."

— Julia Woodruff

"I feel the greatest reward for doing, is the opportunity to do more."

— Dr. Jonas Salk

"Always demanding the best of oneself, living with honor, devoting one's talents and fits to the benefits of others – these are the measures of success that endure when material things have passed away."

— Gerald Ford

"To get what you want, stop doing what isn't working."

— Dennis Weaver

"Look at a day when you are supremely satisfied at the end.
It is not a day when you lounge around doing nothing; it is when you've had everything to do and you've done it."

— Margaret Thatcher

"The secret to joy in work is contained in one word – excellence.
To know how to do something well is to enjoy it."

— Pearl Buck

"The sports page records people's accomplishments, the front page usually records nothing but man's failures."

— Earl Weaver

"Finish each day and be done with it. You have done what you could. Some blunders and absurdities no doubt crept in; forget them as soon as you can. Tomorrow is a new day; begin it well and serenely and with too high a spirit to be encumbered with your old nonsense."

— Ralph Waldo Emerson

"One person with a belief is equal to ninety-nine who have only interests."
— John Stuart Mill

"If life were measured in accomplishments, most of us would die in infancy."
— A.P. Gouthey

"All labor that uplifts humanity has dignity and importance and should be undertaken with painstaking excellence."
— Martin Luther King

"It is those who have this imperative demand for the best in their natures, and who will accept nothing short of it, that holds the banners of progress, that set the standards, the ideals for others."
— Orison Swett Marden

"Death comes to all, but great achievements build a monument which shall endure until the sun grows cold."
— George Fabricius

"Success is not the key to happiness. Happiness is the key to success. If you love what you are doing, you will be successful."
— Albert Schweitzer

"If you want to achieve excellence, you can get there today. As of this second, quit doing less-than- excellent work."
— Thomas Watson

"Mere longevity is a good thing for those who watch life from the side lines. For those who play the game, an hour may be a year, a single day's work an achievement for eternity."
— Gabriel Heatter

"Anything you do, you better enjoy it for its value. Because people are going to second-guess everything you do."
— Bill Gates

"Make it a life-rule to give your best to whatever passes through your hands. Stamp it with your manhood. Let superiority be your trademark."

— Orison Swett Marden

"Every worthwhile accomplishment, big or little has its stages of drudgery and triumph; a beginning and a victory."

— Unknown

"I want to put a ding in the universe."

— Steve Jobs

"Achievement is the knowledge that you have studied and worked hard and done the best that is in you. Success is being praised by others. That is nice but not as important or satisfying. Always aim for achievement and forget about success."

— Helen Hayes

"Great things are not accomplished by those who yield to trends and fads and popular opinion."

— Charles Kuralt

"Do a little more each day than you think you possibly can."

— Lowell Thomas

EPILOGUE

Teams that have developed the right kind of pride and are motivated by love and respect develop an openness of value and persist through difficulties. They understand, accept and embrace their roles, and maintain a positive attitude. When a person makes the decision to join in a team effort, the wisest choice that individual can make is to sacrifice all the superficial self-interest, and to commit his specialized skills to the building of the group.

Hopefully every person involved in athletics at any level will get the opportunity to experience being on a *great team* at least once during their life. Teams provide coaches with unforgettable moments, and help define each individual's focal responsibility as a coach. On a team where all participants are aligned toward a common, clearly defined goal, and are willing to tackle challenging tasks, much can be accomplished. With a sense of friendship and loyalty to each other, plus a personal responsibility for the outcome, a positive, productive atmosphere can be established.

Great teams are made up of individual athletes who have consciously given up their quest for personal glory, who have willingly and wholeheartedly embraced the character traits of a team player, and who have fully committed themselves to the group effort. Over time, these players will come to understand one of life's great lessons—they are a stronger individual if they having experienced being part of a great team. This lesson is one of a coach's greatest legacies.

ABOUT THE AUTHOR

Bruce Eamon Brown is a special presenter for the NAIA's "Champions of Character Program." Previously, he served as the athletic director at Northwest College in Kirkland, Washington. A retired coach, he worked at every level of education in his more than three decades of teaching and coaching. His coaching experiences included basketball, football, volleyball, and baseball at the junior high and high school levels, and basketball at the junior college and college levels. He was involved with championship teams at each level of competition.

Brown is a much sought-after speaker, who frequently addresses coaches, players, and parents on selected aspects concerning participation in sport. He has written several books, including the highly acclaimed *1001 Motivational Messages and Quotes for Athletes and Coaches: Teaching Character Through Sport.* He has also been the featured speaker on several well-received instructional videos:

- Coaching Youth Basketball: Volume 1 – Essentials of Individual Defense
- Coaching Youth Basketball: Volume 2 – Team Defense
- Coaching Youth Basketball: Volume 3 – Fast Break, Early Offense, Press Offense
- Coaching Youth Basketball: Volume 4 – Fundamentals of Zone Offense
- Fun Ways to End Basketball Practice
- Team Building with Positive Conditioning
- The Role of Parents in Athletics
- Redefining the Term "Athlete"
- Teaching Character Through Sport

Brown and his wife, Dana, have five daughters, Allison, Katie, Shannon, Bridget, and Dana. The family resides in Redmond, Washington.